The Blacksmith's Source Book

An Annotated Bibliography

By James Evans Fleming

Southern Illinois University Press

Carbondale and Edwardsville

Library of Congress Cataloging in Publication Data

Fleming, James Evans.
   The blacksmith's source book.

   Bibliography: p.
   Includes indexes.
   1. Blacksmithing--Bibliography. I. Title.
Z6153.B55F56 1980 [TT220] 016.682   80-18560

   ISBN 0-8093-0989-0

Dedicated to Alex and Frank

Contents

Preface

The 276 books and pamphlets listed here, some of which are from the foreign language literature, are those judged to be the most useful to practicing smiths, historians, ironwork enthusiasts, and students. Although a few of the items listed are from private collections, most are found in the Library of Congress.

The material is divided into four parts that are further divided into chapters arranged alphabetically by author.

Part 1 introduces texts, manuals, and courses on the basic processes of blacksmithing and metallurgy.

Part 2 presents more specialized and advanced processes of blacksmithing, including ornamental ironwork, farm smithing, industrial forging, bladesmithing, and works on pattern welded "Damascus" steel.

Part 3 lists books on blacksmithing as a literary and historical subject, focusing primarily on the traditions, lore and descriptions of the various trades in blacksmithing. Several books on the processes, tools, and products of the art are also listed.

Part 4 treats products of the forge from tools and utensils to architectural works, including a special chapter on books emphasizing individual smiths and their work.

Also included are an author index and a title index.

I owe a great deal of thanks to many people who have helped make this book possible, including the National Endowment for the Arts, the office of Congressman Timothy Wirth of Colorado, the staff of the Library of Congress, Vivi Hatch, Slim Spurling, Jean Chen, Hillary Loring, Randall Colver, Bill Wasson, Dan Gift, Frank Turley, Roger Phillips, Dona Meilach, Lance Freudiger, and my parents.

James Evans Fleming

Bonanza, Oregon
April, 1980

Part One

Practical Blacksmithing

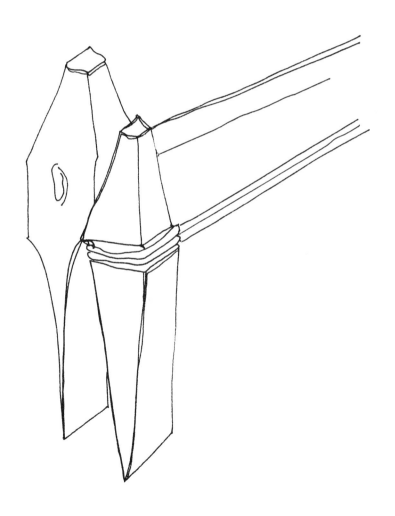

1. Textbooks

At the turn of the nineteenth century many secondary schools, colleges, and trade schools offered courses in basic blacksmithing. Texts were written for these courses by the instructors themselves or by smiths writing for the student market. As a result, a large number of excellent texts were produced. Although some barely introduce the subject while others merely rearrange previously published matter or make direct copies thereof, most texts offer original and useful material to the literature.

Generally the texts are organized in much the same way, first introducing the tools, materials, and equipment and then presenting projects that require the student to use them. In a few cases the course affords some fairly sophisticated projects.

Ashcroft, C. C., and Easton, J. A. G. General Shopwork. Toronto: Macmillan Co. of Canada, 1940.

This is intended as a high school industrial arts course text with a chapter on forge work (pp. 119-27). It briefly surveys the equipment and tools of the forge and discusses the operations of fire

building, cold and hot cutting, squaring, rounding,
swaging, fullering, bending flat and round steel,
punching, bending an eye, forge welding, tempering
tool steel, and case hardening. Projects to exem-
plify the lessons consist of a welded ring and a
cold chisel. A very brief, but fairly inclusive
treatment of the common forge tools and their uses
is included here. It is of use to the student or
instructor as a teaching aid. 239 pp., ill., ind.

Bollinger, Joseph Walter. Elementary Wrought Iron.
Milwaukee: Bruce Publishing Co., 1930.

This basic text uses the method of teaching the
operations by making various projects. It begins
with discussions of the equipment, tools, and
materials, followed by discussions of the operations of bending, twisting, drawing out, cutting,
shaping, fastening, and stock calculations. The
second half of the book is devoted to sixty-eight
projects, most of which involve forgings, such as
andirons, furniture, simple tools, and fireplace
accessories. The designs are of the simplest type
but the fabrication techniques seem sound and could
serve as a guide and source of ideas for more advanced pieces. While not outstanding as a textbook, the work does offer some unique tips. 139
pp., ill., ind.

Buffalo Forge Co. Modern Equipment for Schools of
Mechanical Technology. Buffalo, 1916.

This is basically a catalogue of the Buffalo
Forge Company with a short blacksmith course included. The first section contains descriptions
of Buffalo forges, blowers, punches, drill presses,

anvils, vises, the Beaudry Peerless power hammer, and woodworking tools. Tables and specifications are included where appropriate for determining the right size and type of equipment for a particular job.

The second section of the book is a twenty-exercise blacksmithing course covering basic forging operations, forge welding, chain making, and tong making. Although the explanations are brief the illustrations are good and the information sound.

The last section of the book is entirely made up of photographs of school and industrial shops using Buffalo equipment. All in all, this is an interesting and unique publication, and valuable as an aid and reference work to the student and practicing smith. 95 pp., ill.

Coleman, George J. Forge Notebook. Milwaukee: Bruce Publishing Co., 1921.

This small work gets right to the point and covers much material in a concise, step-by-step manner. The emphasis is strictly on operations rather than projects. It covers tools, equipment, materials, stock calculations, forging operations, and heat treatment. This is a very good introductory treatment of blacksmithing, though in no way adequate as a complete course. 26 pp., ill.

Cross, John Alfred. Metal Forging and Wrought Ironwork: A Manual for Schools. London: Mills and Boon, 1967.

An excellent modern treatment of the smithy and its operations, this book is designed for use in a school industrial arts shop and seems to be influenced by the Council for Small Industries in Rural Areas (CoSIRA) series in some areas, particularly in scroll forming.

The book begins with a survey of the tools, materials, and equipment, with an especially valuable chapter on the making of many shop tools such as tongs, stake tools, special dies, scroll and twisting wrenches, and a butcher. This information is presented in working drawings, photographs, and step-by-step instructions. The second section deals with the basic operations of stock calculation, heats, drawing, pointing, upsetting, cutting, bending, punching, forming large circles, and fire welding.

A third section of the book covers many ornamental elements and operations, including various scrolls, basket handles, feet, splitting, and collaring. An unusually complete treatment includes drip pans, many kinds of leaves, flowers, and buds, all presented in drawings and working explanations. Also unusual and of interest are chapters on repoussé work and design.

This book is well written and illustrated, and is very useful both to the student and the smith. It would make an excellent textbook for a course on ornamental wrought iron. 177 pp., ill., bibliog., ind.

Crowe, Charles Phillip. Forgecraft. Columbus, Ohio: R. G. Adams and Co., 1913.

This basic text of forge work, with good photographs of operations, covers tools, equipment, and

materials adequately. Projects are single forgings, such as grab hooks, gate hooks, and bolts,
intended to introduce the operations rather than
emphasize the projects. The book also covers
stock calculations, metallurgy, heat treating and
forge welding, and contains many tables and charts.
It approaches blacksmithing from an early twentieth-century scientific viewpoint, although practical treatment of forge practice is comparatively
brief. Large sections of the book explain how ore
is made into steel and its metallurgy in somewhat
outdated terminology. Although too brief in many
aspects to be considered a good course, it is full
of information, nevertheless. 175 pp., ill., ind.

Googerty, Thomas Francis. Practical Forging and Art
Smithing. Milwaukee: Bruce Publishing Co., 1915.

The first section of this text teaches basic
blacksmithing from the tools and equipment to shop
layout, basic operations, and simple projects.
This section covers welding, heat treatment and
the making of steel. Projects include tongs,
chain, rings, hooks, and chisels.

The second section addresses itself to various
ornamental projects, including leaves, scrolls,
handles, hinges, and lanterns. Operations cover
repoussé and an unusual and informative section on
chiseling, chasing, and perforating.

Both sections contain much useful knowledge for
both the beginning and the practicing smith. 146
pp., ill., ind.

Harcourt, Robert H. <u>Elementary</u> <u>Forge</u> <u>Practice</u>: <u>A</u>
<u>Text-Book</u> <u>for</u> <u>Technical</u> <u>and</u> <u>Vocational</u> <u>Schools</u>. Palo
Alto, Calif.: Stanford University Press, 1917. 2d
ed., 1920; 3d ed., 1938.

This text/course combination is intended to
train vocational and trade school students in the
various operations of forging iron and steel. The
text introduces each area, be it basic operations,
forge welding, or heat treatment of iron and steel,
and follows each with a series of graduated jobs
designed to apply the principles covered.

The 3d edition (Peoria: The Manual Arts Press,
rev. and enlarged, 1938, 182 pp.) discusses the
manufacture of wrought iron and steel, including
alloys; the effects on grain size of forging the
metal at various heats; and the metallurgy of
steel, including the use of heat-treating equipment.

The second half of the book deals with the manufacture and heat treatment of iron and steel as
understood in the 1930s. This section also contains a description of tools and equipment and a
very brief chapter on power hammers. Each chapter
is followed by study questions. This book does
very well as an aid to learning basic forge techniques, the emphasis being on the principles
rather than the projects.

The projects include staples, a gate hook, tongs,
chain, bolts, chisels, punches, lathe tools, hammers, and a hunting knife. 148 pp., ill., bibliog., ind.

Hughes, Thomas P. Principles of Forging and Heat Treatment of Steel. Minneapolis: Burgess-Roseberry Co., 1928.

This general smithing textbook was written for college-level courses. It covers forge shop equipment, smithing operations of drawing out, upsetting and shouldering, stock calculations, and forge welding. It contains a section on furnaces and fuels, followed by a survey of mechanical forging devices, including presses, upsetting machines, power hammers, and power-hammer tooling.

A survey of iron- and steel-making processes is followed by a discussion of heat treatment, including annealing, hardening and tempering, quenching baths, carburizing, case hardening, and testing of hardness.

Except for a lack of attention given to hand forging operations, the book is a fairly complete basic blacksmithing text, useful to the smith and student for the wide range of material covered and the variety of examples given. 87 pp., ill.

Hundeshagen, Hermann. Kleinschmiede Arbeitsmittel und Verfahren. Berlin: Verlag Technik, 1971.

This technically oriented basic blacksmithing text is written in German. It covers the fundamental operations of drawing, tapering, bending, welding, shouldering, tenon forming, punching, and heat treatment, and contains elaborate sets of formulas for stock calculations for all the operations. It would be valuable to the German-speaking smith or student, but it is sparsely illustrated

and consequently of little value to others. 180
pp., ill., ind., in German.

Ilgen, William Lewis. Forge Work. Editorial revision
by Charles F. Moore. Cincinnati: American Book Co.,
1912.

This comprehensive textbook of basic blacksmithing and forging contains both background information and projects.

Beginning with a survey of the tools and equipment of the smithy, the book then thoroughly covers various types of hammer blows for such operations as upsetting, drawing, tapering, and straightening; this is followed by fire building, welding,
and twisting. A section of practice exercises
includes staples, hooks, chain hooks, welded chain
links, and other welds to illustrate the previously
covered operations. The heat treatment of tool
steel is followed by tool projects and stock calculation, including tongs, chisels, set tools,
hardy tools and calipers. A very good section on
power-hammer tools and operations is followed by a
chapter on scroll forming and collaring. The book
concludes with two chapters on iron and steel making. This good beginning text is adequate to teach
the fundamentals of forging and welding with some
supplemental help. 210 pp., ill., tables.

International Correspondence Schools. <u>Fireproofing</u>
<u>of</u> <u>Buildings,</u> <u>Stair</u> <u>Building,</u> <u>Ornamental</u> <u>Metalwork,</u>
<u>Builders'</u> <u>Hardware,</u> <u>Roofing,</u> <u>Sheet-Metal</u> <u>Work,</u> <u>Mill</u>
<u>Design</u>. I. C. S. Reference Library series. Scranton,
Pa.: International Textbook Co., 1909.

This is a multivolume textbook written for students of architecture, metal working, and the
building trades in the early twentieth century.
Of interest to the blacksmith are the sections on
stair building, ornamental metal work, and wrought
iron applications on and in buildings.

The section on ornamental metal work begins with
a discussion of the tools and applications of cold
bent strap ironwork. Many examples are given, including some construction details. Considerations
of forged work include leaves and foliated work,
and scroll forming, with some explanations of the
processes involved. The operations considered
are applied to elevator enclosures, railings,
gates, window guards, balconies, lamps, and cano-
pies. Special attention is given to circular
staircase design and supporting gates.

The book stresses good design, function, and
aesthetics. While not fully inclusive, the material offers guidelines and applications of use to
the smith and student of architectural blacksmithing. 93 pp., ill.

International Correspondence Schools. Shop Equipment, Hand Forging, Tool Dressing. Scranton, Pa.: International Textbook Press, 1916.

This is really three separate books bound into one volume. Each one is a complete course with study questions and an exam.

Shop Equipment covers practically every common tool and machine used in the early twentieth-century blacksmith shop, with an engraving and an explanation of each article used. Covered are several types of forges, furnaces, tuyeres, tongs, set tools, hammers, anvils, bench and floor tools such as swages, mandrels, and vises, as well as various fuels. Other than the fact that only four types of tongs are described, the information is very complete and useful. 51 pp., ill.

Hand Forging, part 1 deals with the very basic skills such as judging heat, striking, drawing, bending, upsetting, and twisting by making a staple, gate hook, bolt, and a chain hook. Also included is a discussion of steel and iron manufacture. 37 pp., ill.

Hand Forging, part 2 contains a very good section on different types of forge welding, including chain links and tongs. It also contains an interesting section on different ways of making right-angle bends with square corners. Massive industrial forge weldings of locomotive reverse shafts and valve yokes are also discussed. 35 pp., ill.

Tool Dressing deals with the manufacture and properties of tool steel, including forging and heat treatment. The section covers hammers, planer and lathe tools, drill bits, and chisels. It also discusses the welding of steel to iron by cleft and lap welding. 47 pp., ill.

Jernberg, John. Forging: Manual of Practical Instruction in Hand Forging of Wrought Iron, Machine Steel, and Tool Steel; Drop Forging; and Heat Treatment of Steel, Including Annealing, Hardening, and Tempering. Chicago: American Technical Society, 1918.

This manual covers a wide range of subjects which the early twentieth-century blacksmith would deal with. A survey of different types of power hammers, upsetting machines, presses, and cranes follows descriptions of the more common hand tools. A very clear section on forge welding is followed by discussion of forge operations and stock calculations. There is a very good section on power hammer tools and techniques. The final section of the book deals with heat treatment of steel, including case hardening and testing. This is a valuable general manual, particularly to the practicing smith, with its treatment of the power hammer. 131 pp., ill., ind.

Jones, Lynn Charles. Forging and Smithing: A Book for Schools and for Blacksmiths. New York: The Century Co., 1924.

This textbook of practical and farm blacksmithing, with some ornamental projects, is presented in a three-part descriptive fashion. The first section deals with the tools, equipment and fuel of the early 20th century blacksmith shop. The usual tools and equipment are presented, as well as measuring devices, a chapter on drilling, and a section on tapping holes.

The second section deals with the shop and its processes, and includes layout, stock calculation, finishing, a discussion of tool smithing, and some ornamental techniques, such as leaves and basket handles.

The third section applies the principles covered in the first two sections with step-by-step directions for projects ranging from hooks and tongs to chains, basket handles, and hammers. This section also includes the unusual topics of tire setting, babbitting bearings, and plowshare sharpening. Each chapter has study questions and the end of the book contains thirty-five tables, including geometric calculations, weights of various sized steel bars, drill sizes, nail, screw, and bolt specifications, and hardening and tempering charts, making this a very good basic blacksmithing text. 230 pp., ill., tables, ind.

Krom, Edward F., and Paige, Peter J. Hand-Wrought Ironwork: A Book of Projects. Milwaukee: Bruce Publishing Co., 1946.

This high school industrial arts class project book of simple ornamental ironwork executions includes working drawings, instructions, and a photograph of each of fifty-five finished pieces. The projects, such as candelabra, plant stands, tables, lanterns, and lamps, require minimal forging and smithing techniques. Although little or no forging technique is described, this book is useful to the student and smith working on more advanced pieces for design and construction considerations. 111 pp., ill., ind.

Littlefield, James Drake. Notes for Forge Shop Practice: A Course for High Schools. Springfield, Mass.: The Taylor-Holden Co., 1910.

This is a short course set up as a series of job information sheets to supplement an instructor. It covers seventeen jobs ranging from hooks and tongs to punches and a hammer. The jobs are arranged in order of increasing difficulty with new material preceeding each job in which it is needed. The notes also cover fire welding chain and other types of welds. Tools, equipment and materials are covered briefly and there is a section on heat treatment, also brief. While not adequate as a beginning course in itself, it does have merit as a supplemental teaching aid. 69 pp., ill.

Ludwig, Oswald A. Metalwork: Technology and Practice. Bloomington, Ill.: McKnight and McKnight Publishing Co., 1947.

This general high school shop text is intended to introduce a variety of subjects to the student. It contains three sections applicable to the smith.

The first section covers the basic forge hand tools and their uses. The second section deals with the basic smithing operations of drawing out, bending, tapering, twisting, upsetting, forge welding, and making spirals and scrolls. The third section deals with the principal concepts of heat treatment.

This is a very brief treatment of the subject amounting to little more than an illustrated set

of definitions. It would be of some use to the beginner, and to the instructor setting up a course
in basic smithing. Pp. 283-99, ill.

Luehring, Arthur H. Job, Operation, and Information
Sheets for Forge Practice. Terre Haute: Indiana State
Teachers College, 1941.

This work contains a series of beginning projects
presented in step-by-step form intended to be used
with an instructor. The illustrations are lacking
in quality but the text for each project is very
thorough. The jobs include staples, chain links,
and a gate hook. Operations include stock calculations, using the anvil tools, riveting, bending,
and shouldering. Finally there are one- to two-
page information sheets on finishing, heat treating, grinding, and measuring. Each unit has questions and references. Since the original is in
mimeographed form it seems that the course was
presented in loose sheet form for each exercise.
This is common-sense basic blacksmithing supplement most helpful used with an instructor but detailed enough to suffice for an individual. 152
pp., ill.

Lukowitz, Joseph J. Interesting Art-Metal Work. New
York: Bruce Publishing Co., 1936.

This is a school shop course project book of
simple cold bent ironwork executions presented with
working drawings and step-by-step instructions. The
projects include various candle and flower pot
holders. Supplemental information is provided on
raising and sinking sheet copper for ashtrays and
trays. It contains some useful tips and good ideas

but generally is unsuited to the smith. 63 pp.,
ill.

Ortega, Juan B. <u>Blacksmithing</u> <u>Practices</u>. Washington,
D. C.: International Cooperation Administration,
1957.

   This manual describes the tools and equipment of
a nonelectrical smithy with brief explanations of
forging operations such as welding, fire-building,
and general methods. It discusses the practical
considerations of shop set-up and layout. It would
be useful to the student as a general introduction
to the components of the smithy. 26 pp., ill.

Richards, William Allyn. <u>Forging</u> <u>of</u> <u>Iron</u> <u>and</u> <u>Steel</u>: <u>A</u>
<u>Text</u> <u>Book</u> <u>for</u> <u>the</u> <u>Use</u> <u>of</u> <u>Students</u> <u>in</u> <u>Colleges</u>, <u>Second-</u>
<u>ary</u> <u>Schools</u> <u>and</u> <u>the</u> <u>Shop</u>. New York: Van Nostrand Co.,
1915.

   Set up in textbook rather than course outline
form, this work addresses itself to the operations
and principles of blacksmithing rather than to
specific jobs. The illustrations are hand-drawn
and pleasing to look at. Many unusual hand tools
are described in the tool and equipment section as
well as anvils, forges, and several types of forge
fires. Most of the standard forge operations are
covered, including forge welding and heat treatment. A section on carbon steels and metallurgy is
followed by a chapter on the power hammer and a
chapter on some ornamental topics such as tools,
scrolls, spiral twists, and methods of fastening
pieces together. An appendix, consisting of forty-
two jobs such as chain links, chisels, gate hooks,
nails, hoisting hooks, lathe tools, and ice tongs

in step-by-step fashion referring back to the text,
is followed by a few tables. Each chapter concludes
with review questions. The book is a fairly complete basic course and should be interesting and
informative to practicing smiths and students
alike. 219 pp., ill., ind.

Schuster, Hans, and Kirchner, Karl. Grundlagen des
Freihandschmiedens: Eine Einfuhrung in die Techniken
mit 50 Arbeitsblattern. Stuttgart: Robert Kohlhammer,
1956.

The ability to read German would be an undoubted
asset in using this book but the illustrations are
good enough to offer a great deal without further
explanation. The book is set up in course form
and deals with the forming of simple forgings and
the operations involved. Its value to the English-
speaking smith lies in variations of already
familiar processes and it is not recommended for
the novice as a beginning text. The projects include hinges, tongs, chisels, scroll work, and
basket handles. Operations include bar piercing,
right-angle bends, and shouldering. Of particular
interest is the attention given to positioning the
work on the anvil and the direction of hammer
blows. 50 pp., ill.

Schwarzkopf, Ernst. Plain and Ornamental Forging. New
York: John Wiley and Sons, 1916.

This is a high school textbook of beginning and
intermediate forging. It opens with a discussion of
the materials, tools, and equipment of the smithy.
The basic techniques and operations are set forth
by making a series of projects, including hooks,

nails, bolts, various welding exercises, tongs, and rings.

A chapter on steel is followed by information on heat treatment, which is applied to making punches, chisels, hardies, and lathe tools.

A chapter on more advanced forgings follows with such exercises as andirons, engine parts, and power-hammer work. An outstanding section on art forging finishes the text with instructions for making spirals, scrolls, leaves, and roses from the solid. An appendix offers information on such subjects as finishing, coloring, brazing, and soldering metal.

The book deserves better illustrations and more discussion in some areas but it remains one of the best basic blacksmithing books written, and is important to the smith and student. 292 pp., ill., tables, ind.

Selvidge, R. W. Blacksmithing. Peoria, Ill.: The Manual Arts Press, 1925.

Containing no projects as such, this text emphasizes the many operations of blacksmithing in forty-eight steps, beginning with the basics, such as fire building, drawing out, bending, upsetting, punching, and fullering, and continuing with heat treatment, welding, striking, and case hardening. Related shop skills are also covered, such as riveting, bending pipe, babbitting, filing, and saw sharpening. Fourteen of the operations apply especially to farm blacksmithing and include such items as setting wagon and buggy tires, renewing wagon felloes and spokes, sharpening and pointing plowshares, and fitting horseshoes.

The second part of the book supplies the body of information needed to apply the operations and includes setting up the shop, explaining the tools, equipment, and materials, the different types of fluxes, fires, and fuels. The book concludes with several tables.

As might be expected, a book of this small size, in attempting to cover so much material, is necessarily brief and in fact is only barely adequate in some areas. It is, however, a good introduction to the state of practical blacksmithing of this period and offers up much information with a little effort. Each item is followed by references and good study questions. 155 pp., ill.

Shirley, Alfred James, and Shirley, Alfred Frank. Handcraft in Metal: A Text Book for the Use of Teachers, Students and Craftsmen. London: B. T. Batsford, 1953.

This is a general school shop text covering a variety of subjects that include sheet-metal work, casting, and some machining. The chapter on forging, welding, and heat treatment (pp. 63-88) is considered here.

The first section of this chapter deals with the operations of drawing down, bending, upsetting, swaging, fullering, and punching, which are presented as definitions with minimal descriptions of the processes involved. This section is followed by a survey of the blacksmith's hand tools, forge, gas and electric welding, and heat treatment. The

last section consists of exercises, including ring
bending, punches, chisels, hooks, handles, and
pokers. Several novel ideas for handles are presented but otherwise the chapter is too brief and
shallow to be of much aid to the student or smith.
244 pp., ill., ind.

Smith, Robert Ernst. Units in Forging and Welding.
Wichita, Kans.: McCormick-Mathers Publishing Co.,
1941.

   This is a very basic course in elementary forge
operations, including gas and arc welding. The
first twenty-five pages deal with forging and begin
with a description of the tools, equipment, and
materials. Fire building and the different forging
operations, including forge welding and heat treating, follow. Set up in units with step-by-step instructions, this book would be a valuable aid in
teaching an introductory blacksmithing course
when used with other material. 56 pp., ill.

Underwood, Austin. Creative Wrought Ironwork. London:
B. T. Batsford, 1965.

   This is a beginning text geared to the modern
school shop. It covers a wide range of projects
with photographs and explanatory text and good
attention is given to particulars of technique.
Beginning with simple fire tools, the author quick-
ly moves into scrolls. Unusual in this kind of
book is the fabrication of scrolls into fire
screens, lamps, and trivets using rivets and collars. The author uses gas brazing and welding
freely, only mentioning fire welding. He also
avoids fullering, swaging, and upsetting, consid-

ering them too complicated for the beginner. While
not standing wholly on its own as a complete introduction to blacksmithing, the book does offer
the student and smith many workable ideas, techniques, and tips. 96 pp., ill., bibliog., ind.

2. Self-taught Courses

This small yet distinct group of books is intended for the home craftsperson to use without the aid of supplemental instruction to gain knowledge and insight into the field of blacksmithing. Although the overall quality of the books reflects the knowledge of each author, several are excellent and would prove a welcome addition to any smith's library and each one offers its particular approach to accomplishing various projects.

Council for Small Industries in Rural Areas. The Blacksmith's Craft: An Introduction to Smithing for Apprentices and Craftsmen. London: 1952.

This is an excellent basic blacksmith course set up in lessons with photographs and text intended to teach the student or novice elementary blacksmithing.

Part 1 describes the equipment, tools, fire building, and materials; it also defines operations such as heating, drawing out, bending, upsetting, cutting, punching, drifting, and forge welding.

Part 2 is a series of elementary exercises set forth with step-by-step photographs and accompanying descriptions. These lessons include forging a taper, staples, "S" hooks, a gate hook, chain links, and a holdfast.

Part 3 emphasizes stock calculation in a series of lessons including forge welding of rings and chain, and the forging of hoisting hooks, shackles, cotters, bolts, and harrow bars and tines.

Part 4 further develops dimension forging and welding with such projects as round and square corner bends, various welds, tongs, and rivets.

This is perhaps the best book of basic forge practice ever written for self-teaching blacksmithing. The photographs are excellent. It is recommended as a basic text for novices and students, as well as a reference book for practicing smiths, owing to the variety of projects covered. 104 pp., ill., bibliog.

Danielle, Joseph Williams. Early American Metal Projects. Bloomington: McKnight and McKnight, 1971.

This textbook intended for high school shop classes consists of very simple projects of Colonial American design including casting, tinwork, lathe work, and simple forge work. Considered here is a chapter of fireplace hardware designs (pp. 23-42). Projects presented with scale drawings and instructions on construction procedure include fire tools, a fireplace crane, a trammel, fire dogs, andirons, and several trivets. While the procedures utilize a minimum of forge work, the drawings are accurate enough to be used as patterns and can be applied by the smith using traditional techniques. 145 pp., ill.

Flint, James W. Metalwork Practice. London: B. T. Batsford, 1963.

This is a step-by-step course, with about thirty projects, for the modern metal shop. The only blacksmithing involves forging a taper on a chisel and making a screwdriver. It relies heavily on drilling, chiseling, filing, and cold bending. This book has very little to offer the practicing or aspiring smith, being more intended for a high school industrial arts course. 96 pp., ill.

Pehoski, Joe. Blacksmithing for the Home Craftsman. Washington, Tex., 1973.

This little book serves well as a kind of primer for more elaborate treatises on blacksmithing. The emphasis here is on operations rather than particular projects. It covers shop layout, tools and equipment, fire building, judging heats, forging a taper and point, heat treatment, and several kinds of fire welds including chain links. It covers the making of a chisel, tongs, and a hardy cut. Of particular interest to the student is the attention given to troubleshooting poor heat treatment and blown welds. 44 pp., ill., bibliog.

Available from Iron Heart Forge, Box 313, Washington, TX 77880.

Savage, Robert H. Pennsylvania German Wrought Ironwork. Home Craft Course, vol. 10. Plymouth Meeting, Pa.: Mrs. C. Naaman Keyser, 1947.

This small pamphlet is intended to introduce construction techniques for some common ironwork of

the Pennsylvania German blacksmith to the novice.
First, it briefly discusses the material, equipment, and tools for setting up a basic shop. Then
it describes the fuels and fire building. Next it
covers the operations of cutting, twisting, upsetting, drawing, welding, and punching. Projects
such as tenons, nails, hinges, trivets, and fire
tools are each presented on a well-illustrated
page showing the different steps of construction,
further explained with marginal notes. This is an
interesting and informative introduction to Pennsylvania German ironwork, valuable to the smith
but not complete enough for the novice as the projects are too hard for a beginner. 33 pp., ill.,
bibliog.

Weygers, Alexander G. The Making of Tools. New York:
Van Nostrand Reinhold Co., 1973.

This is home craft text intended to introduce
the student to basic tool shaping, heat treatment
and finishing. The equipment used would probably
exist in a modern smithy or could easily be ob-
tained or fashioned by the craftsperson.

Operations covered include heat treatment, grinding, polishing, and some hot forming on the anvil.
Projects include garden tools, pliers, gouges,
hammers, chisels, and hooks.

Useful techniques, such as fitting handles and
sharpening gouges and chisels, are covered. This
book offers much practical information on tool
making, useful to the smith and to the student for
its unique and practical applications. 93 pp.,
ill.

Weygers, Alexander G. The Modern Blacksmith. New
York: Van Nostrand Reinhold Co., 1974.

This basic toolsmithing text with many techniques
and operations unique to the author's own personal
experience is oriented toward the home shop. It
covers shop tools and equipment, use of the hammer,
and fire building, as well as the basic operations
of tapering, drawing, upsetting, bending, and heat
treating of steel with such projects as punches
and chisels.

The book then illustrates the decorative forging
of rosettes, scrolls, hinges, and door latches.
The making of useful blacksmith hold-down tools,
tongs, fire tools, bicks, hammer heads, and a
small anvil from railroad iron are well explained.
Projects include woodworking and stonecarving
tools.

The projects are well thought out, clearly explained and well illustrated, offering many new
ideas and techniques strongly emphasizing the re-
cycling of used materials for equipment and stock.
While the book falls short of being a complete
blacksmithing text, its supplemental value to the
practicing smith, student, and home craftsperson
is considerable. 96 pp., ill.

3. Manuals of Basic Blacksmithing

These manuals were written as a means for practicing smiths to broaden their knowledge of various
aspects of blacksmithing by presenting an overview of
the processes, descriptions of the tools and equipment, and background material on alternate methods
and techniques. Generally the manuals listed here go
somewhat beyond elementary blacksmithing, at times
including descriptions of the tools, equipment, and
operations typical of the textbooks, but with less
emphasis on the graduated projects so applicable to
the classroom. For the most part they deal with projects that the practicing smith, is likely to face in
working situations. Also included in this section
are the perfunctory treatments of the tools and processes usually found as chapters in "home handyman"
books.

Almeida, Oscar. <u>Metalworking</u>. New York: Drake,
1971.

> This is a general metal techniques manual cover-
> ing a variety of processes, including blacksmith-
> ing and heat treatment. It is intended to

familiarize the nonstudent with a broad spectrum of the metalworking field.

"Blacksmithing", pp. 93-110, briefly describes materials, tools, equipment, and the operations of drawing, flaring, bending, twisting, upsetting, and punching. Explanations are given for the use of punches, flatters, fullers, and swages.

"Heat Treatment of Steel", pp. 111-26, offers an explanation of hardening and tempering, covering a few of the techniques and some of the pitfalls of the practice, which is followed by a metallurgy section which includes more definitions of terms.

This book offers an introductory discourse on blacksmithing and heat treatment too brief to be of much use to the student or practicing blacksmith. 204 pp., ill., ind.

Anderson, Edwin P. Audels Millwrights and Mechanics Guide: For Plant Maintainers, Builders, Riggers, Erectors, Operators, Construction Men, and Engineers. New York: Theo. Audel and Co., 1940.

This is brief survey of the hand tools of the smithy, illustrating many tongs and set tools. Some equipment is illustrated but the emphasis is on hand tools. Discussions of operations are rudimentary and brief, including upsetting, bending, shouldering, cutting, and punching. In no way is this book comprehensive, but it is accurate and adequate enough to help an isolated novice if no better material is on hand. Pp. 153-98, ill.

Andrews, Jack. <u>Edge</u> <u>of</u> <u>the</u> <u>Anvil:</u> <u>A</u> <u>Resource</u> <u>Book</u> <u>for</u>
<u>the</u> <u>Blacksmith</u>. Emmaus, Pa.: Rodale Press, 1977.

This excellent manual of practical blacksmithing
is intended for both the practicing blacksmith and
the student.

Section 1 deals with blacksmithing as an art/
craft and discusses marketing, records keeping,
planning executions, sketching and drawing, record-
ing finished pieces, and developing a portfolio.

Section 2 covers the layout of the shop and its
tools, equipment, and materials.

Section 3 explains the operations of fire building, cutting, drawing out, twisting, heat treating,
upsetting, heading, welding, splitting, fullering,
swaging, and striking, in such projects as fire
tools, punches, chisels, a chain hook, spoons,
nails, tongs, hinges, hammers, and anvil tools.
This section also includes the techniques of making spirals, collars, knives, and chain links.

Section 4 covers heat treatment, metallurgy,
stock calculations, spark testing, finishing, and
various formulas for coloring, pickling, and carburizing.

Section 5 is a series of photographs of the forge
work of Samuel Yellin from the Yellin Museum in
Philadelphia.

Addressing itself well to the new generation of
blacksmiths, this book is full of practical information useful to the student and practicing smith.
210 pp., ill., tables, bibliog.

Bacon, John Lord. Forge Practice and Heat Treatment
of Steel. New York: John Wiley and Sons, 1908.

This voluminous manual is one of the better basic
blacksmithing books. It covers the same ground as
most similar manuals but more thoroughly. A discussion of the basic tools is followed by chapters
on welding, stock calculation, and basic forging
operations. Simple forgings of a gate hook, chain
hook, and tongs are followed by an excellent chapter on power hammer work and a chapter on tool
forging and tempering. A very extensive discussion
on steel and iron, heat treating furnaces, more on
heat treatment and case hardening completes the
text. A series of tables is followed by working
drawings of forge projects.

The book needs more illustrations but it is well
written and easy to read. It would be useful to
the practicing smith as a reference manual, particularly for heat treatment and power-hammer
tooling. 418 pp., tables.

Bacon, John Lord. "Forging," in Cyclopedia of Modern
Shop Practice. Edited by Howard M. Raymond. Chicago:
American Technical Society, 1915.

This basic blacksmithing manual covers many
essentials of the trade. A survey of the tools
and equipment is followed by descriptions of the
fire and of forge welding. The operations of drawing, punching, stock calculation, power-hammer
work, and heat treatment are applied to the manufacture of chain, tongs, a ladle, bolts, chisels,
punches, hammers, and lathe bits. Power-hammer
tooling is covered for various types of hammers

and basic power-hammer forging operations are described. Pp. 261-358, ill.

Bacon, John Lord, and Johnson, Carl Gunnard. Forging: A Practical Treatise on Hand Forging of Wrought Iron, Machine Steel, and Tool Steel; Drop Forging; and Heat Treatment of Steel, Including Annealing, Hardening, and Tempering. Chicago: American Technical Society, 1933.

This practical treatise is intended to provide background information on metalsmithing from the manufacture of the raw materials to the physical effects of forging on various types of steel.

The first section describes the manufacture of iron and steel and the several processes and chemical reactions in each. This section covers the structure of steel, including the ingot, and the effect of carbon and impurities and grain growth. It also contains a spark identification chart and a metallurgical discussion.

The second section covers the hand tools of the blacksmith shop and various power hammers, with a good section on power-hammer tools and processes. More unusual is a brief discussion of upsetting machines and rolling mill equipment. Part 2 begins with sections on the metallurgical and physical effects of forging, including grain flow diagrams and the effects and defects of heat and forging on grain size. This section concludes with a discussion of defects in forging, welding, and refining.

A section on drop forging using dies is followed by a discussion of cold forging and its effect on grain size and shape. The final section of the book covers heat treatment, with the making of chisels as examples.

Over all, this is a scholarly and valuable book for the student, professional smith, or instructor. It contains a wealth of practical and useful information not readily observable in the smithy but very important to good workmanship. 115 pp., ill., ind.

Bealer, Alex W. The Art of Blacksmithing. New York: Funk and Wagnalls, 1969.

This overview of blacksmithing is intended for the general reader to put blacksmithing into a historical perspective and to record some of the techniques of the trade.

The beginning of the book contains a survey of blacksmithing through antiquity, the production of iron and charcoal, and some of the tools and equipment of the shop. Next the techniques of bending, welding, drawing out, punching, upsetting, and heat treatment are covered, followed by the making of such tools as hammers, tongs, files, axes, and a shovel. Next, the making of hardware, including nails, hinges, hasps, and doorknockers, is followed by the process in setting wagon tires. A section on fire tools, andirons, and fireplace implements is followed by decorative animal heads, flowers and leaves, and scroll work. A chapter on making weapons concludes the technical passages.

An interesting book, covering a wide range of forge work, written in a discursive style which makes it difficult to use by the practicing smith

yet too technical to be considered as general
reading. 438 pp., ill., bibliog., ind.

Bryne, Oliver. The Practical Metal Worker's Assis-
tant. New York: H. C. Baird, 1882.

In its day this was a definitive practical treatise of the state of the art of iron and steel
manufacture. It is very thorough in the treatment
of fluxes, chemical processes as understood, and
the design of the smelting and blacksmithing
equipment of the day.

A second section covers the forging operations
of the smithy, the fire and tools of the shop, and
the making of several jobs, including bolts and
nuts. Also in this section is an interesting discussion of various power hammers, particularly
the water-powered tilt hammer.

The third section discusses forge welding, including scarfing, pipe and barrel welding, damascus
twist barrels, chain, hatchets, and the welding of
steel to iron. This section also covers the use
of heading tools, swages, punches, and trip hammers.

The final section of the book is on the heat
treatment of steel. Although it is lacking in
sound metallurgical science, it does seem accurate
on the whole and is the more interesting because
everything is presented in the nontechnical terms
of analogy, geared to produce the right results
without fully understanding why.

This book is important to the historian as a
rare treatment from this period containing much
practical information about subjects deleted as
outdated by later blacksmithing manuals. It is

valuable to the historian, practicing smith, and
student. 577 pp., ill.

Casterlin, Warren S. Steel Working and Tool Dressing:
A Manual of Practical Information for Blacksmiths and
all Other Workers in Steel and Iron. New York: M. T.
Richardson, 1914.

This practical blacksmithing compendium of useful information is intended for blacksmiths and
tool smiths. The material is presented in topical
form offering methods of heat treatment, designs
of smithing tools, tips on running the smithy, and
much lore and advice from the author's fifty-seven
years of experience. Many forging jobs which deal
with steel are presented, including steeling axes,
making a drawknife, welding, and making tongs.
The book contains a great deal of useful and
accurate information for the practicing smith.
207 pp., ill., ind.

Doke, Clement Martyn. The Lambas of Northern
Rhodesia: A Study of Their Beliefs and Customs.
Westport, Conn.: Negro University Press, n.d.

This study contains a chapter (pp. 347-51) on
primitive Rhodesian blacksmithing, including a
description of the equipment and processes and a
summary of the duties of the smith. Ill.

Drastík, Frantisek. Volné rucní kování: Druhé nez-
menené vydáné. Prague: Nakladatelstvé Technické
Literatury, 1971.

This basic blacksmithing manual also contains
illustrations of tools, equipment, and basic forging operations. Projects, including a three-tined

pitch fork, chain links, tongs, a hammer head, and
horseshoe nails, are all useful and several are
made with unusual techniques. The text is in
Czechoslovakian but the illustrations are self-
explanatory and require no captions. 100 pp., ill.

Hasluck, Paul Nooncree. Smith's Work. New York:
Cassell and Co., 1902.

This is almost identical to Morton's An Expert
Blacksmith's Manual of Blacksmithing, published in
Chicago the same year. Hasluck has added more
illustrations, emphasizing brand names of equipment more than Morton's Manual does. While Hasluck
is the editor, no mention is made whatever of
Morton's involvement in the material. 160 pp.,
ill., ind.

Hawley, J. E. The Blacksmith and His Art. Pheonix,
Ariz.: J. E. Hawley, Publisher, 1976.

This exhaustively researched book, dedicated to
preserving and furthering blacksmithing, touches
on almost every area of the subject.

The book begins with a chronological development
of the smith as recovered by archeology from earliest finds to the building of Rome. At that
point the author departs from the scientific and
relys on references in the humanities, notably in
Greek and Roman mythology, the Bible, poetry,
painting, woodcuts, and sculpture. The importance
of iron to Roman civilization, to the Moslems of
Persia and Syria, to Mediaeval Europe, and to
Renaissance Europe is covered in terms of its
religious, utilitarian, and military applications.
Smith guilds and apprenticeships are followed

throughout their history to the present, and important smiths and groups of smiths are described.
The development of smithing in America is followed
from Colonial times to the decline of traditional
blacksmithing in the early twentieth century.

A chapter on basic tools and equipment of the
shop and shop set-up is followed by general smithing instructions which the author presents as
eight basic, separate operations. The operations
are: fire control and taking a heat, drawing down,
bending and bending jigs, piercing, cutting, forge
welding, and heat treating. Each operation is
accompanied by projects which explain the applications. A chapter on the design considerations of
art smithing completes the text.

The author presents many photographs of European
and American architectural ironwork, and artisti-
cally executed hardware, furniture, and implements.

A directory of blacksmith suppliers is followed
by reprints of several modern supply catalogs and
an annotated bibliography.

This is an excellent resource book for the
blacksmith, apprentice, and historian. The
author's love of his craft abounds, the historical
references are carefully researched, and the general instruction is both informative and useful.
176 pp., ill., tables, bibliog., ind.

Holmstrom and Holford. American Blacksmithing,
Toolsmith and Steel Workers' Manual. Chicago: F. J.
Drake and Co., 1916.

Of all the books written by Holmstrom this one
is the most eloquently spiced with philosophy,

advice, and opinion. In terms of length and scope
this book was his most ambitious attempt at expres-
sion. Written for the practicing blacksmith, both
authors explain too little about a lot of topics
and leave the reader wanting clearer explanations
and more thorough instructions. Much good advice
is spread among a mass of verbiage in chapters and
sections which are not clearly organized.

American Blacksmithing, by Holstrom, begins with
a series of articles expressing the author's personal opinions of blacksmithing's relationship to
such areas as religion, temperance, smoking,
guilds, unions, taxation, big government, literacy,
and the state of blacksmithing in general, all
giving an interesting and sometimes amusing insight
into the concerns of those times. Next the book
explains the shop, tools, and equipment briefly
and then follows with a series of paragraphs on
various subjects such as welding iron, drilling
chilled iron, sewing drive belts, and dressing
axes, drills, and stone tools. A chapter on wagon
tires is followed by two chapters on plowshares,
then followed by more short articles on such unrelated topics as babbitting, drilling, saw mending,
and boiler work. The remainder of the book discusses horseshoeing and the horse's foot.

The Twentieth Century Toolsmith and Steelworker,
presumably by Holford, begins with an explanation
of such terms as heating, forging, hammering, heat
treatment, and welding, followed by advice on
judging steel and its hardness. The next several
chapters discuss the shop, its tools and equipment,

and offer advice on the making of some of the hand
tools of the smithy. A chapter on such common
articles as picks, axes, and knives is followed by
a series of chapters, each relating to the making
of the tools of different trades. These include
machinists' tools, such as rivet snaps and calking
tools; woodworkers' tools, including chisels and a
draw knife; stone cutters' tools for limestone,
granite and sandstone; miners' tools such as rock
drills and reamers; and the tools of the farrier,
harnessmaker, butcher, and railroad worker. The
final section of the book deals with special tricks
of hardening and tempering tools, followed by formulas for various heat treatment compounds and
more receipts.

This book is difficult to use and the organization can be trying when one attempts to recover a
certain piece of remembered information. It does,
however, offer a wealth of interesting information
and is an important source of unusual processes
for the smith patient enough to study it. 456 pp.,
ill.

Joseph, Charles, and Bocquet, J. A. Le Serrurier:
expose methodique des connaissances pratiques et
theoriques indispensables aux serruriers. Paris:
Justin Storck, n.d.

This French text is of interest to English-
speaking smiths for the thirty-five plates depicting a variety of tools, techniques, and products of the smith. Iron- and steel-making facilities are diagrammed, followed by tools and equipment of the forge, including the bellows, vise,

power hammer and drill press. The operations of
drawing, upsetting, shouldering, cutting of intricate cross-sections of stock, punching, riveting,
and scroll forming are covered, followed by the
technique of gate hanging and door hardware fastening. 35 plates plus text in French.

Lillico, J. W. Blacksmith's Manual Illustrated: A
Practical Treatise on Modern Methods of Production
for Blacksmiths, Apprentice Blacksmiths, Engineers
and Others. London: The Technical Press, 1930.

This book for smiths is intended to provide information and ideas on a variety of operations and
tools. It offers the most complete treatment of
trip hammer tools and operations ever published,
and so is an excellent source of information in
this area.

Other topics covered include stock calculations,
forge welding, and heat treatment. A variety of
projects are explained, including axes, wrenches,
hinges, hooks, and chain links. Valuable knowledge is provided for the forging of complicated
pieces in a series of illustrations with accompanying text.

While the illustrations are not the most aesthe-
tic possible, the information is clear and sound.
Valuable to everyone seriously interested in smithing, particularly to the production smith as an
educational reference work. 213 pp., ill., tables.

Moore, Thomas. Handbook of Practical Smithing and
Forging: The Smith and Forgeman's Handbook. New
York: Spon and Chamberlain, 1906.

This practical treatise is intended for the use
of blacksmiths rather than students. The first
section covers the equipment, tools, and materials
of the forge, followed by a chapter on steel manufacture and testing.

The second part of the book deals with various
forgings, such as hoisting hooks, yokes, cotter
pins, washers, wrenches, rings, and scrolls. In-
terspersed with these forgings are discussions of
supplemental tools, such as set tools, scroll forms
and bending jigs. The material in this section is
presented textually with infrequent illustrations.
A glossary of technical and nontechnical blacksmithing terms is provided, followed by tables.

This book is not well organized and is difficult
to use effectively. It does have a great deal of
information and would yield much of value to a
patient and persistent smith, particularly in the
intermediate area between industrial and practical
blacksmithing. 248 pp., ill., tables, ind.

[Morton, C. S.] Manual of Modern Blacksmithing.
Chicago: Gerlotte Publishing Co., 1902.

This basic blacksmithing treatise is intended to
aid blacksmiths in, and to introduce students to,
the smithy. It begins with a survey of the equipment and hand tools of the forge, including a good
description of a foot-powered Oliver type of power
hammer. Next covered are the operations of drawing down, upsetting, punching, welding. A chapter

on the structural considerations of forging, including grain size and flow, is followed by a section on bending and ring-making, including multi-
ple weldings on rings and bridles. Two chapters
on examples of forge work include tie rods, eccentric rods, chain links, a swivel, and a crankshaft, as constructed both with and without the
use of a power hammer. A chapter on making two
homemade portable forges is followed by a section
on heat treatment of steel.

   The book offers some unique and well-considered
information for the smith; the ideas on shop equipment and tools are particularly usable. 158 pp.,
ill., ind.

Nicholson, Peter. Mechanic's Companion. London:
Bartlett and Hinton, 1825.

   This voluminous treatise includes a brief survey
of the smithy and its processes that is intended
to introduce the novice to the blacksmithing field.
The chapter "Smithing" (pp. 415-45) contains a
description of the forge, its tools and equipment,
followed by the operations of taking a heat, punching, cutting plate, making screw bolts, and riveting. The chapter concludes with a discussion of
the extraction of iron from its ore and the making
of steel. It is interesting as an early source of
information on the blacksmithing process. Ill.

Richardson, Milton Thomas, ed. <u>Practical</u> <u>Blacksmith-</u><u>ing</u>: <u>A</u> <u>Collection</u> <u>of</u> <u>Articles</u> <u>Contributed</u> <u>at</u> <u>Differ-</u><u>ent</u> <u>Times</u> <u>by</u> <u>Skilled</u> <u>Workmen</u> <u>to</u> <u>the</u> <u>Columns</u> <u>of</u> <u>"The</u> <u>Blacksmith</u> <u>and</u> <u>Wheelwright"</u> <u>and</u> <u>Covering</u> <u>Nearly</u> <u>the</u> <u>Whole</u> <u>Range</u> <u>of</u> <u>Blacksmithing</u> <u>from</u> <u>the</u> <u>Simplest</u> <u>Job</u> <u>of</u> <u>Work</u> <u>to</u> <u>Some</u> <u>of</u> <u>the</u> <u>Most</u> <u>Complex</u> <u>Forgings</u>. 4 vols. 1889-1891. Reprint (4 vols. in 1). Foreword by Dona Z. Meilach. New York: Crown Publishers, Weathervane Books, 1978.

Volume 1 begins with a brief history of iron-working and early tools of blacksmithing, and con-tinues with shop plans, designs of equipment, and descriptions of the basic tools. This volume also contains useful information on anvil and saw-blade mending. 224 pp., ill., ind.

Volume 2 begins with a history of iron making, followed by a consideration of the products, wrought iron and steel. Steel is discussed with respect to heat treatment, workability, and test-ing, including case hardening. A chapter on bolt slippers and rivet making is followed by a section on chisels, their uses and abuses. The subject of drilling, drillpresses, and drifting is then cov-ered, including several designs for homemade drills. Next the area of fullering and swaging, including the use of top and bottom dies, is pre-sented along with the types of tools and opera-tions commonly used. The next chapter presents a variety of odd jobs and tools of the smith, in-cluding tool repair, cranes, and several wheel-wrighting aids. The volume concludes with dis-

cussions on shears, grinding, and emery wheels.
262 pp., ill., ind.

Volume 3 continues the descriptions of hand tools
and also presents some specialized tools for plowshare work. A chapter on wrenches is followed by
a section on welding, brazing, and soldering. The
working and heat treatment of steel, including the
case hardening of iron, is then presented, with
special attention given to the practical considerations of both common and unusual jobs. The next
two chapters describe a variety of complicated
forging jobs, some industrial, with no regard to
fundamental smithing. The final chapter presents
one of the most detailed discussions on plowshare
work ever written. 307 pp., ill., ind.

Volume 4 contains much information for the
wheelwright and carriage ironer, including tire
setting, axle setting, spring making, and the
manufacture of various carriage irons. A unique
chapter on the making of bobsleds is followed by a
section on the tempering of various tools. The
next chapter covers the considerations of bolt and
nut making, followed by chapters on welding and
case hardening. This volume closes with a section
of tables. 276 pp., ill., ind.

The entire four-volume series is presented in a
topical form, reasonably well-organized and read-
able. Notably absent are basic smithing techniques
and work under the power hammer. Over all, this
is an excellent resource book for the practicing
blacksmith and wheelwright.

Simmons, Marc, and Turley, Frank. <u>Southwestern</u> <u>Colo</u>-
<u>nial</u> <u>Ironwork</u>: <u>The</u> <u>Blacksmithing</u> <u>Tradition</u> <u>from</u>
<u>Texas</u> <u>to</u> <u>California</u>. Sante Fe: Museum of New Mexico
Press, 1980.

 This book presents a survey of blacksmithing
processes, applications, and development in the
Colonial Southwest. The European origins are followed into Mexico and from there through the
Southwest. A section on the tools and techniques
of frontier smithing and farriery is followed by a
survey of the smith-made implements, hardware, and
tools, including those for domestic, religious,
and military applications.

Spon, E., and Spon, F. N. <u>Spons'</u> <u>Mechanics'</u> <u>Own</u>
<u>Book</u>: <u>A</u> <u>Manual</u> <u>for</u> <u>Handicraftsmen</u> <u>and</u> <u>Amateurs</u>. 6th
ed. New York: Spon and Chamberlain, 1907.

 This large general shop handbook is intended for
craftsmen and home handimen and contains a chapter
on forging and finishing. It defines the terms
and operations of smithing and illustrates and
explains the tools and equipment of the forge.
Different uses of specialized chisels are included
and drilling, filing and threading are all covered.

 A section on heat treatment and an explanation
of the smith's materials is followed by a series
of examples of forgework. These include keys,
bolts, nuts, tongs, hammers, chisels, file finishing, scrapers, drifts, punches, wrenches, and
spanners. Often several alternative methods of
construction are considered, depending on the
tools available. An interesting section on
straightening warped sheet and plate stock by
hammering concludes this section.

Though not complete, this treatment of forgework is unusual in its slant toward the machinist. Offers good information to the smith not found elsewhere. Pp. 44-90, ill.

U. S., War Department. The Blacksmith and the Welder. Technical Manual TM 10-440. Washington, D. C.: Superintendent of Documents, 1941.

Only the first thirty pages of this manual apply to forging. The majority of this section is devoted to the tools and equipment of the traditional smithy with additional paragraphs discussing heat treatment, fire building, drawing, bending, stock calculations, and considerations of forge welding. Although it is useful as an illustrated definition of terms, it is not adequate as a course. 97 pp., ill., bibliog.

Westover, Ozro A. The Scientific Steel Worker: A Practical Manual for Steel Workers and Blacksmiths: The Art of Working Steel Thoroughly Explained, Also Steel Working Receipts and Mechanical Tables for Making Rings of All Sizes of Iron, Steel and Angle Iron. Wheeling, West Virginia: Wheeling News Litho Co., 1906.

This excellent practical manual is intended to instruct the smith in forging and finishing tools made from various tool steels and alloys. It begins with a description of the types of various tool steels, how carbon affects them, and how the method of forging changes with each.

A series of projects follows, including chisels, hammers, twist drills, and a butcher knife. The

author goes to great lengths to explain proper
heating, forging, and handling.

The subjects of annealing, hardening, tempering,
and heating methods are next discussed both generally and in reference to specific projects, including anvils, hammers, punches, dies, and
machine tools.

Sections on welding, brazing, and case hardening
complete the general text, which is followed by
brief essays on a variety of subjects, including
furnace building, recutting old files, acid etching, drilling chilled cast iron, and making holes
in glass. Various formulas are presented for
welding compounds, hardening compounds, hardening
and tempering baths. Tables of circumference and
area of circles are followed by the chapter on
working angle iron and making rings that concludes
the book.

This is well-written but poorly organized book
full of pertinent solutions to old questions. It
offers a good working knowledge based on practical
experience, and is valuable to the blacksmith and
student, as well as the aficionado for its anec-
dotal lore. 199 pp., ill, tables, ind.

Wormald, Tom. Blacksmith's Pocket Book, Broadway
Engineering Handbook, vol. 32. London: Scott, 1921.

This is a small book of industrial forgings and
shop advice for the smith and his helper. It contains instructions and diagrams for making hoisting hooks, shackles, brake straps, levers, "T"
rods, and various engine components, both with the
steam hammer and with hand tools. It contains a

section on press forging into dies, and a section
on wagon ironing, including the making of levers,
eye bolts, and spring hoops. It concludes with
advice to the foreman and the would-be foreman.

This is an interesting approach to industrial
shop work useful to the smith with a power hammer.
87 pp., ill., ind.

4. Reference Works for Smiths

This section concentrates on books covering special aspects of smithing of use to practicing smiths. Some of the books listed deal specifically with blacksmithing subjects, such as forge tools, making equipment, selecting tool steels, hanging gates, and installing architectural ironwork. Other practical knowledge is also presented here, including tool use, nonsmithing metalworking techniques, foreign styles of blacksmithing, and design. Of special interest to practicing smiths are books of tables and formulas of the trade. The diverse information covered here is important in providing background skills and techniques not usually found elsewhere in the blacksmithing literature.

Aston, James, and Story, Edward B. <u>Wrought</u> <u>Iron: Its</u> <u>Manufacture, Characteristics and Applications</u>. Pittsburgh: A. M. Byers Co., 1941.

This work examines the manufacture and uses of wrought iron through history and explores the usefulness of this material in the steel age.

It contains detailed analyses of early samples of wrought iron and a historical survey of all methods of its extraction from iron ore, including the modern methods. The book establishes quality standards and surveys both the characteristics of wrought iron and its uses in place of steel. 59 pp., ill.

Barr, Archibald. The Value of Science in the Smithy and Forge. Introduction by William Hutton Cathcart. Edited by John Edward Stead. London: Charles Griffin and Co., 1916.

This manual of practical information for working blacksmiths is intended to supplement the trade with material on topics usually overlooked in other manuals.

It contains sections on stock calculation, estimating forging dimensions for a given strength requirement, formulas for pattern making from sheet or plate, practical geometry, heat treatment, welding chemistry, and case hardening.

This is a valuable handbook for blacksmiths with little engineering training, as the applications explored in this book are both simple and useful. 163 pp., ill., ind.

Bearss, Edwin C. Blacksmith Shop: Lyndon B. Johnson Historic Site. Historic Structure Report and Furnishing Study. Denver: National Park Service, 1973.

This pamphlet is a detailed account of the physical layout and tooling of a nineteenth-century Southwest blacksmith shop, compiled from available literature, interviews, and out-of-print books. It describes the shop, its equipment, and the tools

suitable for smithing, wheelwrighting, and horseshoeing. 26 pp., ill., bibliog.

Bethlehem Steel Corporation. <u>Modern</u> <u>Steels</u> <u>and</u> <u>Their</u>
<u>Properties:</u> <u>Carbon</u> <u>and</u> <u>Alloy</u> <u>Steel</u> <u>Bars</u> <u>and</u> <u>Rods</u>.
Handbook no. 2757. Bethlehem, Pa.: 1972.

This handbook of Bethlehem Steel Corporation
products includes their specifications, uses, and
heat treatment.

The majority of the book consists of working data
for each type of steel the company makes, including
composition, heat treatment procedures, and effects
of different heat treatments on the physical characteristics of the material. Background information
includes an explanation on ways of steel making,
types of steels, and the effects of alloying elements. Tables break down the many alloys into
specialized areas according to use, giving composition and AISI nomenclature. A section on the
varying ability of steels to harden includes an
explanation of the tests used and a table of the
results on a variety of specimens. A glossary of
heat treatment terms is followed by methods of
heat treatment for a number of alloys.

This is a useful reference book for the smith
desiring more exotic steels for special purposes.
208 pp., ill., tables, ind.

Blossfeldt, Karl. <u>Urformen</u> <u>der</u> <u>Kunst</u>. Tübingen: Ernst,
Wasmuth, 1933.

This book comprises a photographic study of
plants from a design point of view. It presents
forty-nine species of herbs, shrubs, and trees in
black and white closeup photographs which emphasize

the details of design aesthetics, notably symmetry,
found within nature. Fritz Kühn refers to this
study as a major influence in his own work. Many
of the examples bear an uncanny resemblance to
ironwork; so closely, in fact, that it appears the
author had such a relationship in mind, thus presenting a fertile ground of ideas for the black-
smith-designer to apply and develop. 133 pp., ill.,
text in German.

Carpenter Steel Division. Working Data: Carpenter
Stainless Steels. Reading, Pa.: Carpenter Technology
Corporation, 1973.

This is a catalogue of stainless steels produced by this company. The steels are arranged
according to application, including improved corrosion resistance and increased strength. Each
steel's characteristics are given, including uses,
corrosion resistance, physical properties, recommended heat treatment, workability, and forms
available.

It contains supplemental sections on corrosion,
physical constants, ability to take a weld or be
forged, cleaning, finishing, mechining, forming,
and polishing of stainless steel.

The catalogue is useful as a reference guide to
many types of stainless steels and their applications. 182 pp., ill., ind.

Council on Small Industries in Rural Areas. <u>Metals</u>
<u>for</u> <u>Engineering</u> <u>Craftsmen</u>: <u>A</u> <u>Guide</u> <u>to</u> <u>Their</u> <u>Composi-</u>
<u>tion,</u> <u>Properties,</u> <u>and</u> <u>Manipulation</u>. London: Benham
and Co., 1964.

This handbook is intended to introduce crafts-
persons to the properties, uses, and characteristics of a variety of metals. These include cast
iron, wrought iron, high-carbon steel, high-speed
and special alloy steels, and the nonferrous metals
including aluminum, aluminum alloys, copper, copper alloys, various brasses, and several bronzes.
In all, over forty metal compositions are discussed. It is of value to the practicing smith as
a reference work to aid in the selection of ferrous and nonferrous metals. 69 pp., ill.

Hommel, Rudolph P. <u>China</u> <u>at</u> <u>Work</u>. New York: 1937.
Reprint. Cambridge, Mass.: M.I.T. Press, 1969.

This account of early Chinese industry describes
the tools, processes, and products of a variety of
undertakings. Of interest to the blacksmith are
sections on Chinese blacksmithing tools, nailmak-
ing, and ornamental examples, including andirons.
In addition, many iron and steel tools used in
farming, housekeeping, and crafting are illustrated. 366 pp., ill., ind.

Intermediate Technology Development Group Project,
Zambia. <u>Oil</u> <u>Drum</u> <u>Forges</u>: <u>Bellows</u> <u>Operated,</u> <u>Fan</u> <u>Oper-</u>
<u>ated</u>. London: Intermediate Technology Publications,
n.d.

This booklet gives detailed plans for construction of two types of forges, one bellows-operated
and the other blower-operated. The projects are

designed to be made within the capability of a
minimally equiped shop with simple tools and non-
specialized, readily available, materials. 40 pp.,
ill.

Kolchin, B. A. _Metallurgy_ _and_ _Metalworking_ _in_ _Ancient_
Russia. Jerusalem: Israel Program for Scientific
Translations, 1967.

This historical treatise on the metalworking
techniques and products of ancient Russia diagrams
and explains the processes of furnace building,
ore extraction, and steel making on a very basic
level. Tools of the smith are described, as are
the processes of forging, heat treatment, grinding, soldering, and plating.

Products of the smith are examined in detail
with regards to structure, probable method of manufacture, and variations through time. Knives,
agricultural tools, weapons, armor, locks, and
craftsmans' tools are covered in this manner. The
book concludes with a general overview of the
blacksmith industry and the many diverse trades
which specialized from it between the ninth and
thirteenth centuries in Russia.

This is an interesting and useful study of intermediate technology processes in the developing arts
of blacksmithing valuable to the historian, the
smith, and the student for background information
in this basically unchanged field. 112 pp., ill.,
ind.

Kronquist, Emil F. Metalwork for Craftsmen. Originally
published as Art Metalwork. 1942. Reprint. New York:
Dover Publications, 1972.

This is a basic homecraft introduction to working nonferrous metals with descriptions of processes used as applied to fifty-five projects.

Techniques and processes include annealing,
pickling, raising, planishing, soldering, chasing,
repoussé, and etching. Projects include a variety
of holloware and flatware pieces. It would be useful to the practicing smith as a supplemental
reference work in metal working. 202 pp., ill.,
ind.

Marquardt, Julius. The Smith's Pocket Companion: Con-
taining Useful Information and Tables on Iron and
Steel, for the Use of Smiths and Steel Workers.
Duluth, Minn.: N.p., 1893.

This reference handbook for blacksmiths contains
tables of dimensions and weights of various iron
bars and pipes, steel balls, selected metals and
other substances; nail, screw, and bolt sizes;
engineering specifications for bearing weights of
pins; mensuration; properties of alloys and compositions; and decimal equivalents of inches. Sections are included on steel and iron manufacture,
furnace and forge design and use, heat treatment,
and forge welding. Many receipts are given for
hardening, tempering, case hardening, and welding
compounds. This is a useful reference book for
practicing blacksmiths. 136 pp., ill., ind.

Murphy, H. G. <u>Hammered</u> <u>Metalwork</u>. Foreword by Franklin
T. Evans. London: University of London Press, 1936.

This is a thorough, well-organized manual of
many sheet-metal working processes and techniques
usually associated with silversmithing. It contains chapters on the tools and equipment; the
materials, copper, brass, and silver; techniques,
including raising, sinking, cutting, planishing,
hinging, finishing, soldering, and polishing; and
projects with step-by-step instructions which include bowls, pots, boxes, trays, and a candlestick.
The material is clearly written and detailed enough
to learn from without an instructor. 259 pp., 76
pls.

Nicholson File Co. <u>File</u> <u>Filosophy</u>: <u>And</u> <u>How</u> <u>to</u> <u>Get</u> <u>the</u>
<u>Most</u> <u>Out</u> <u>of</u> <u>Files,</u> <u>Being</u> <u>a</u> <u>Brief</u> <u>Account</u> <u>of</u> <u>the</u> <u>His</u>-
<u>tory,</u> <u>Manufacture,</u> <u>Variety,</u> <u>and</u> <u>Uses</u> <u>of</u> <u>Files</u> <u>in</u> <u>Gen</u>-
<u>eral</u>. Providence, R. I.: N.p., 1956.

This information booklet covers a variety of
aspects of files and their uses. Topics include
the history of file-making, steps in modern file-
making, types of files and their uses, and how to
use a file properly in various applications and
for various materials. It contains a glossary of
file terms, instructions for file care and saw
sharpening with files. This is a useful booklet
for getting the maximum service from this often
misused tool. 50 pp., ill.

Parker, Thomas Netherson. An Essay on the Construction, Hanging, and Fastening of Gates. London: Lackington, Allen and Co., 1804.

This well-studied essay on the principles of gate hanging includes the calculations necessary to erect a gate that will swing of its own accord through a preplanned arc to rest in a certain open or closed position. It is intended for all gates, whether of wood, wrought or cast iron. It covers hinge, thrust bearing, and catch design and positioning. While somewhat archaic in language, the information is all there for this unique treatment of a common architectural blacksmithing problem. 116 pp., ill.

Sallows, James Francis. The Blacksmith's Guide: Valuable Instructions on Forging, Welding, Hardening, Tempering, Casehardening, Annealing, Coloring, Brazing, and General Blacksmithing. Brattleboro, Vt.: Technical Press, 1907.

This manual of instruction in working steel is intended as a reference work for the practicing smith. It contains sections on tool forging, heat treatment, and alloy forgings. The first section, on machine forging, covers the production of various tools used in working with lathes and other machinery, the making of engine components, and the technique of forge welding. Tool forging is the subject of the second section, which includes the making of chisels, lathe tools, and weldless rings.

A section on heat treatment describes the process and gives instructions for the heat treatment

of various tools and steel parts. This section is
followed by chapters on working high speed steel,
coloring and case hardening iron, brazing, and
some tips useful for plowshare and farrier work.
There is an appendix on the design of a furnace.

This is a useful reference book for the practicing smith, particularly in the areas of tool forging, heat treatment, and color case hardening.
168 pp., ill., tables, ind.

Smith, H. R. Bradley. Blacksmiths' and Farriers'
Tools at Shelburne Museum: A History of Their Development from Forge to Factory. Museum Pamphlet Series,
no. 7. Shelburne, Vt.: Shelburne Museum, 1966.

This is basically a catalog of the tools of
Shelburne Museum with explanations as to their
functions. It covers a variety of fire tools,
anvils, hammers, set tools, punches, swages, fullers, power-hammer spring tools, the heavier floor
equipment, and farriers' tools. The text is closely
correlated with the illustrations, which not only
identify the tool but give its use also.

Much additional information is added to this
work to make it even richer. Essays are included
on such topics as the history of iron and steel
use, welding wrought iron and mild steel, and the
hammer. With the use of photographs and step-by-
step instructions the operations of forging a
toasting fork and shoeing a horse are covered.

This is an excellent reference book of tool
identification for the smith and student. 277 pp.,
ill., bibliog., ind.

Teledyne Vasco. <u>Tool</u> <u>and</u> <u>Specialty</u> <u>Steel</u> <u>Guide</u>.
Latrobe, Pa., n.d.

This listing of the products from this steel
maker includes the characteristics, heat treatment
procedures, applications and composition of over
seventy-five types of tool and alloy steels. It is
very useful in the selection of materials for
specific tools and products. 96 pp., ill., tables.

Untracht, Oppi. <u>Metal</u> <u>Techniques</u> <u>for</u> <u>Craftsmen</u>: <u>A</u>
<u>Basic</u> <u>Manual</u> <u>for</u> <u>Craftsmen</u> <u>on</u> <u>the</u> <u>Methods</u> <u>of</u> <u>Forming</u>
<u>and</u> <u>Decorating</u> <u>Metals</u>. Garden City, N. Y.: Doubleday
and Co., 1968.

This general art metal techniques book covers a
wide range of processes and materials intended for
the home craftsperson. It deals with metallurgy of
ferrous and nonferrous metals, forging, repoussé,
etching, soldering, casting, spinning, plating,
and finishing of gold, silver, pewter, and iron,
including the use of hand tools and chemicals.
The section on forging iron is very brief, so the
greatest value to the blacksmith is in the survey
of techniques for other metals and processes. 509
pp., ill., tables, bibliog., ind.

U. S., Library of Congress, Division of Bibliogra-
phies. <u>Elementary</u> <u>Books</u> <u>on</u> <u>Blacksmithing</u> <u>and</u> <u>Forging</u>.
Washington, D. C.: 1940.

This brief bibliography contains annotations of
six basic blacksmithing books intended to aid the
student in finding suitable material for learning
the trade. The bibliography lists Bollinger's
<u>Elementary</u> <u>Wrought</u> <u>Iron</u>, Harcourt's <u>Elementary</u>
<u>Forge</u> <u>Practice</u>, Johnson's <u>Forging</u> <u>Practice</u>, Jones'

Forging and Smithing, Schwarzkopf's Plain and Ornamental Forging, and Selvidge's Blacksmithing, all covered in this Sourcebook. 2 pp.

Viehweger, E. Schlosser-Arbeiten. Berlin and Leipzig: G. J. Göschen, 1915-16.

This is a reference work intended to give architectural ironworkers technical information regarding building and installing stairways, hanging gates and doors, and attaching railings to pillars. Many different hinge and casement arrangements are covered. Designs of various ornamental executions are scattered throughout the book. Much technical information, including formulas, are lost because the text is in German, but the pictures alone make this book a valuable aid to executing architectural ironwork. 131 pp., ill.

Watson, John. Tables for the Use of Blacksmiths and Forgers: Giving the Allowance for Drawing Down and Staving of Round, Square, and Flat Sections of All Sizes, Also Tables for Hoop Lengths, and for the Weights of Iron and Steel Bars, Including Instructions for Estimating the Weights of Forgings. New York: Longmans, Green, and Co., 1906.

This unique reference book contains an elaborate set of tables that enable the blacksmith to calculate the length of stock necessary in a given dimension to produce a certain length of stock of another dimension when forged. It includes tables of weight per foot of round, square, and flat bars, and decimal equivalents of inches. It is particularly useful to the practicing smith working to dimension on complex forgings. 88 pp.

Young, Daniel W. <u>The</u> <u>Practical</u> <u>Blacksmith:</u> <u>Comprising</u> <u>the</u> <u>Latest</u> <u>and</u> <u>Most</u> <u>Valuable</u> <u>Receipts</u> <u>for</u> <u>the</u> <u>Iron</u> <u>and</u> <u>Steel</u> <u>Worker,</u> <u>Steel</u> <u>Welding</u> <u>of</u> <u>Any</u> <u>Kind</u> <u>and</u> <u>Tempering</u> <u>of</u> <u>Any</u> <u>Kind</u> <u>of</u> <u>Tool</u> <u>or</u> <u>Instrument</u> <u>Made</u> <u>Easy.</u> <u>Indis-</u> <u>pensable</u> <u>Information</u> <u>for</u> <u>the</u> <u>Iron</u> <u>and</u> <u>Steel</u> <u>Industry</u> <u>of</u> <u>this</u> <u>Country</u>. Dayton, Ohio: Press of U.B. Publishing House, 1895.

This series of formulas and receipts is intended for blacksmiths as a guide to chemical mixtures for special heat treating applications. It contains forty receipts for a variety of uses, including hardening baths, tempering baths, case hardening compounds, welding compounds, and finishes for iron and steel to protect them from rust.

This is an interesting and useful reference book for the smith. While some of the mixtures seem a bit outrageous, others make more sense and are obviously useful. 36 pp.

5. Metallurgy

One of the most misunderstood areas of blacksmithing is what happens to the atomic structure,
qualities, and characteristics of ferrous and nonferrous metals when heated, cooled, forged, cold
worked, and heat treated, particularly with respect
to their heat treatment. An understanding of the
changes the metal goes through when subjected to
these forces is essential to smithing, particularly
toolsmithing.

The subject of metallurgy has developed so rapid-
ly since the beginning of this century that it comes
as little surprise that few blacksmiths of the earlier
period had more than an empirical knowledge of the
area, based mainly on what worked for them. Information from many of the smithing books of that era are
fraught with conjecture, invented terminology, and
erroneous conclusions. Today quite the opposite is
true, but the effect on the smith is often the same,
one of bafflement and confusion. Today the area is so
intricate, so well defined, that it takes a doctorate
to appreciate the subject fully. However, it is possible to obtain a good working knowledge of the

essentials of metallurgy in a few hours of study,
enough for the smith intelligently to heat, treat and
work the materials. That is the purpose of this chapter, which is not meant to be all inclusive, but to
serve as a guide to the most practical and accessible
sources of information.

Allen, Dell K. Metallurgy Theory and Practice. Chicago: American Technical Society, 1969.

This general metallurgy textbook intended for
college level courses covers a wide subject area.

It begins with a thorough survey of metal-testing
techniques, including spark testing; physical
metallurgy, including grain growth and flow; and
alloy chemistry, including the study of eutectic
mixtures.

The metallurgy of iron and steel is specifically
covered in studies on the effects of heating and
cooling different carbon/iron concentrations; heat
treating methods, effects, and terminology; and a
variety of surface treatments for iron and steel.
Various alloy and tool steel explanations complete
the material directly relevant to the smith.

The remainder of the text deals with cast irons,
nonferrous metals, and the specific metallurgies
of foundry, welding, and machining.

This book is useful to the smith as theoretical
background to more detailed and technical studies
of the metallurgy of iron and steel. 663 pp., ill.,
ind.

Enos, George Magee, and Fontaine, William E. <u>Elements</u>
<u>of</u> <u>Heat</u> <u>Treatment</u>. New York: John Wiley and Sons,
1953.

> This is a college level textbook on metallurgy
> designed for engineering students.
>
> It covers testing equipment, effects of heating
> and cooling on steel, annealing, hardening and tem-
> pering of various types of steel, the effects of
> mechanical working, and surface hardening treat-
> ments.
>
> It also includes heat treatment of cast iron and
> nonferrous metals.
>
> This detailed treatment of the theory and prin-
> ciples of heat treatment emphasizes technical con-
> siderations rather than practical operations. It
> is useful as background information for the smith.
> 286 pp., ill., ind.

Grossman, Marcus Aurelius. <u>Elements</u> <u>of</u> <u>Heat</u> <u>Treatment</u>:
<u>A</u> <u>Series</u> <u>of</u> <u>Educational</u> <u>Lectures</u> <u>on</u> <u>the</u> <u>Principles</u> <u>of</u>
<u>Heat</u> <u>Treatment</u> <u>of</u> <u>Steels,</u> <u>First</u> <u>Presented</u> <u>to</u> <u>Members</u>
<u>of</u> <u>the</u> <u>A.S.M.</u> During <u>the</u> <u>Seventeenth</u> <u>National</u> <u>Metal</u>
<u>Congress</u> <u>and</u> <u>Exposition,</u> <u>Chicago,</u> <u>1935,</u> <u>and</u> <u>Later</u> <u>Ex-</u>
<u>tended</u> <u>to</u> <u>Include</u> <u>the</u> <u>More</u> <u>Recent</u> <u>Developments</u>. Cleve-
land: American Society for Metals, 1935.

> These educational lectures on the principles of
> heat treatment of steel were intended for indus-
> trial engineers and heat treaters.
>
> It contains sections on hardening, normalizing,
> tempering, case hardening, grain size, and the
> iron/carbon diagram.

This very clearly written treatise on many aspects of heat treatment is of use to the smith for
the principles it imparts. 243 pp., ill., ind.

Houghton, E. F. Houghton on Quenching: A Treatise on
the Quenching of Steel, Prepared by the Houghton Metal
Research Staff. Philadelphia, 1943.

This handbook of Houghton quenching media with a
discussion of the general subject is intended as a
simple explanation for industrial heat treatment
facilities. It looks at what happens in the heating and cooling of iron and steel, particularly
with regard to grain growth, changes in chemical
composition, and the properties of hardened martensite. Cooling rates and their effects on the
formation of martensite are discussed. Various
quenching media are discussed with regard to their
advantages, disadvantages, and special uses. The
specific advantages of Houghton's own products are
compared to standard media and the specifications
and uses for those products are given.

This book gives a thorough treatment of hardening media and provides a clear explanation of what
happens in the process. It is useful to toolsmiths
as a practical handbook of heat treatment processes.
69 pp., ill.

Houghton, E. F. and Company. Quenching Media: How the
Houghton Research Staff Made Uniformity Possible with
Oil Hardening. Philadelphia, 1922.

This handbook of various hardening media for
steel is intended to provide the heat treater with
working data on the available substances.

It covers water, oil, Houghton's special oils and water additives, and the effects of each on the speed and severity of the quench of the article being heat treated.

Although it is very brief, it is informative about many aspects of the process. 40 pp., ill.

Houghton, Phillip Stephen. Heat Treatment of Metals: For Manufacturing Processes and Service. 2 vols. Brighton, England: Machinery Publishing Co., 1960.

This thorough handbook is designed for industry to provide working knowledge and principles of metallurgy for heat treaters of tools and machine parts made of all heat-treatable metals.

Volume 1 contains definitions of heat treatment terms and processes, the heat treatment of many nonferrous alloys, including bronze and aluminum; the effects of heat on iron and steel; hardening and tempering; and case hardening and nitriding. 155 pp., ill., tables, bibliog., ind.

Volume 2 contains sections on the ability of iron and steel to harden; the effects of temperature changes on grain size and chemical composition; the processes of annealing, forging, hardening and tempering; special considerations of product and furnace design; and troubleshooting failures. 183 pp., ill., tables, bibliog., ind.

All sections are very well organized and written with no technical applications left out. This work is an excellent source of metallurgical data for the blacksmith seeking a good understanding of the subject.

Industrial Press, The. <u>Heat</u> <u>Treatment</u> <u>of</u> <u>Steel:</u> <u>A</u>
<u>Comprehensive</u> <u>Treatise</u> <u>on</u> <u>the</u> <u>Hardening,</u> <u>Tempering,</u>
<u>Annealing</u> <u>and</u> <u>Case</u> <u>Hardening</u> <u>of</u> <u>Various</u> <u>Kinds</u> <u>of</u>
<u>Steel,</u> <u>Including</u> <u>High-Speed,</u> <u>High-Carbon,</u> <u>Alloy</u> <u>and</u>
<u>Low-Carbon</u> <u>Steels,</u> <u>Together</u> <u>with</u> <u>Chapters</u> <u>on</u> <u>Heat-</u>
<u>Treating</u> <u>Furnaces</u> <u>and</u> <u>on</u> <u>Hardness</u> <u>Testing.</u> New York:
The Industrial Press, 1914.

This comprehensive treatise on the heat treatment of various types of steel is intended as
practical instruction in shops of various sizes.
It contains designs of furnaces for heating with
different fuels; it covers various baths for hardening and tempering steel, including salt baths
and electric furnaces; it discusses case hardening
of mild steel, heat treatments of various alloy
steels; and it surveys various testing procedures,
facts, and recipes to give the smith a wide range
of sophistication and control in heat treatment
processes. 277 pp., ill., ind.

Kamenichny, I. S. <u>A</u> <u>Short</u> <u>Handbook</u> <u>of</u> <u>Heat</u> <u>Treatment.</u>
Translated by I. Savin. Moscow: Mir, 1965.

This reference handbook intended to provide working data to operators of heat treatment shops contains 144 tables plus supplemental text.

It describes heat treatment charts and heat
treatment procedures for various tools and machinery. It also includes a glossary of terms; quality
control; heat treatment of iron, steel, cast iron,
and nonferrous alloys; and case hardening. Specific
tools are exemplified with drawings and detailed
procedures.

It thoroughly covers many aspects of heat treatment practice without going into theory or principles. A drawback is that all grades of steel are
in the Russian classification with no ready cross
reference to the American system. 277 pp., ill.,
ind.

Rogers, Bruce A. The Nature of Metals. Cambridge,
Mass.: M.I.T. Press, 1964.

This technical treatment of general metallurgy
is intended as a college text for readers with a
minimum of scientific background.

It offers all metals, including copper, silver,
gold, and aluminum, their crystalline structure,
their alloys, and the effects on physical characteristics by changing the relative concentrations
of the elements of their alloys.

Two chapters deal with iron and steel metallurgy.
The effects of heating and cooling different compositions of steel leads to a discussion of heat
treatment and the factors affecting hardness and
toughness.

The remainder of the book deals with alloys of
gold and other metals, considerations of deforming
metals, and nuclear reactor metallurgy.

This technically worded treatise is of less value
to smiths than the practical handbooks which deal
more specifically with the metallurgy and heat
treatment of iron alloys. 324 pp., ill., ind.

Rosenberg, S. J., and Digges, T. G. Heat Treatment
and Properties of Iron and Steel. National Bureau of
Standards Circular 495. Washington, D. C.: U. S. Department of Commerce, 1950.

This brief treatment of metallurgy and heat
treatment of ferrous alloys is primarily intended
to provide the uninitiated with a knowledge of the
basic theoretical and practical principles of the
subject. It discusses iron and steel and the effects of heating and cooling on the working properties of grain size, chemical composition and
crystal structure. It covers heat treatment of iron
and steel, including annealing, hardening and tempering, case hardening, nitriding, and special
processes and techniques. A section on the heat
treatment of cast iron is followed by tables on
the classification of steels, their heat treatment
specifications and uses.

This well-written discourse on metallurgy is
useful to the smith desiring a working knowledge
of the subject. 33 pp., ill., tables.

Selander, Einar, ed. Glossary of Heat Treatment: With
Definitions in English and Equivalents in French,
German, Swedish, Russian and Japanese. Stockholm:
Swedish Center of Technical Terminology, 1974.

This booklet comprises definitions of 200 important metallurgical and heat treatment terms in
English translated into five other languages. It
is useful in the translation of works in these
languages, as well as being a good dictionary of
common metallurgical terms in English. 87 pp.

Tobin, James D. <u>Fundamentals</u> <u>of</u> <u>Heat</u> <u>Treating</u> <u>Metals</u>.
Oregon A. S. M., 1970.

This reference book of heat treatment terms and
procedures is primarily intended to give the non-
metallurgist a basic understanding of the subject
and the ability to select the proper heat treatment
sequence for a given product.

It contains a glossary of general metallurgical
and specific heat treatment terms. A section on
hardness includes methods of testing. Sections on
metallurgy include the iron/carbon phase diagram,
the crystalline structure of carbon steels, and a
series of graphs plotting the effects of different
heat treatment processes on grain size and crystal
composition.

Although it is too brief to provide a sound understanding of the processes, it is useful as a
reference to recall specific details, particularly
in the heat treatment of tools. 33 pp., ill.

Part Two

Specialized Areas of Blacksmithing

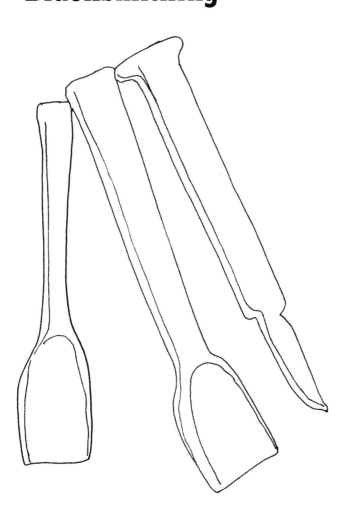

6. Ornamental Ironworking

An important aspect of modern blacksmithing is the adornment and accenting of strictly functional executions with decorative elements. The books listed here present techniques and processes for forging and applying scrolls, leaves and flowers, twists, baskets, and animal heads, among other things. Many books placed in other chapters contain significant contributions to this area, and are so noted.

Bakony, Lucien, and Roviere, Jean. Pratique du fer Forge et de la Ferronnerie Decorative. Paris: Eyrolles, 1965.

> This modern French text of basic ornamental ironwork operations and techniques includes design; scroll pattern making; the forging operations of drawing, bending, twisting, and forge welding, the use of several types of bending jigs, and a chapter on arc and oxy-acetylene welding. The photographs are easily understood but not entirely self-explanatory, so that this book would be of use primarily for the French-speaking student. 126 pp., ill.

Bijlsma, K., and Kok, P. Siersmeden: Een Serie Voorbeelden met Toelichting voor Smeden, Tevens Leidraad Bij Het Zelf Ontwerpen en Maken van Siersmeedwerk. Deventer, Holland: Kluwer Technische Boeken, 1950.

This is a manual of ornamental iron design and construction. It contains many excellent drawings of lamps, fire tools, hooks, brackets, stands, candle holders, chandeliers, andirons, and grill work. Often several examples are presented in each category with construction details illustrated in a few places. The text presumably relates to the construction of the pieces, though a skilled smith would only need the illustrations in most cases. 143 pp., ill., in Dutch.

Council for Small Industries in Rural Area. Decorative Ironwork: Some Aspects of Design and Technique. Publication no. 73. Colchester, Great Britain: Benham and Co., 1973.

This is an excellent book of ironwork designs intended for the practicing smith that suggests avenues of pursuit in designing and executing grills, screens, and gates. Five distinct patterns are given with photographs and captions descriptive of layout, execution, and construction for each. This little work emphasizes calculations and pattern following for duplication of repetitive elements, though tools and operations are described where appropriate.

This is one of few books dealing specifically with advanced ornamental forgework. A book of practical instruction for practicing smiths, it is highly recommended. 79 pp., ill.

Council for Small Industries in Rural Areas. <u>Wrought</u>
<u>Ironwork:</u> <u>A</u> <u>Manual</u> <u>of</u> <u>Instruction</u> <u>for</u> <u>Craftsmen</u>. Pub-
lication no. 55. London: W. S. Cowell, Ltd., 1953.

This excellent book of decorative ironwork, intended for practicing smiths and students involved
with ornamental forgework, presents the techniques
in step-by-step photographs with descriptive captions.

The operations are introduced with a description
of the tools of the ornamental shop that will be
needed, including tongs, set tools, and a monkey
tool.

Part 1 covers the making of scrolls, including
the ribbon, fishtail, solid snub end, half penny,
beveled, and blown-over leaf-type ends. It also
covers a scroll jigging tool for making "S" and
"C" scrolls, followed by a section on collaring,
twisting, making acanthus leaves, and punching
bars for grills and gate rails.

Part 2 describes the construction of a gate and
the forged components that go into it, including
upset heel bars, tenon forming, forge welding mul-
tiple scroll panels, and forging dog bars. It also
covers the fitting, assembly and hanging of the
gate, including setting rivets and collars. It
concludes by discussing various finishes for preserving the completed piece.

This is an essential book for the practicing
smith interested in traditional techniques of the
fabrication and construction of ornamental ironwork. It is also the best treatment in English on
the construction of a gate. 98 pp., ill., bibliog.

Googerty, Thomas Francis. Decorative Wrought Ironwork: Working Drawings and Working Notes on the Making of Simple, Useful Articles from Wrought Iron, Brass and Copper. Peoria: The Manual Arts Press, 1937.

This is a short book of projects, intended to give the practicing smith and student information about the construction of a variety of simple projects. It assumes basic knowledge of smithing and contains no information on the shop or its operations.

Working drawings and instruction for projects such as fireplace tools, candlesticks, hinges, door knockers, lights, and stands for flowers and ash trays, are included.

This book leaves something to be desired in the author's choice of projects but it does offer information on techniques and operations which can be applied by the smith to more interesting executions. 79 pp., ill.

Googerty, Thomas Francis. Hand-Forging and Wrought Iron Ornamental Work. Chicago: Popular Mechanics Co., 1911.

This book is primarily a source of ideas, techniques and projects in decorative ornamental ironwork with only perfunctory treatment of the basic tools, materials, equipment, and operations which include welding, drawing out, and punching.

The main value of the book lies in its treatment of various twists, spirals, baskets, collars, scroll ends, and handles, all of which are clearly explained and illustrated. It contains a section on embossing such projects as acanthus leaves and rosettes, with the tools and techniques used to execute them. There are sections on hinges, drawer pulls, escutcheon plates, and other door hardware. The book concludes with a unique section on iron lamps, their design and construction.

This book is full of good ideas for ornamental projects and offers material not seen elsewhere. It is useful to the student and practicing smith alike. 197 pp., ill., ind.

Haapsalo, Mikko. _Taitava Takoja_. Helsinki: Osakeyhtio Valistus, 1976.

This is a collection of ornamental ironwork techniques and projects for a variety of objects and processes intended for the craftsperson in iron. A display of the common forge tools is followed by a section on ornamental operations, including scroll forming, collaring, splitting, upsetting, twisting, and punching. Sheet-metal working, raising, flame cutting, and fabrication of sculptural pieces are next presented, often accompanied by supplemental photographs showing details of the techniques and operations involved. Examples shown include trivets, candelabra, fireplace tools, and grillwork.

This book is very useful to the smith interested in the ornamental subjects covered. It contains some refreshing and useful techniques, presented in clear photographs which do not need the captions (in Finnish) for comprehension. 98 pp., ill. Text in Finnish.

Hasluck, Paul N. Bent Iron Work: Including Elementary
Art Metal Work. New York: Cassell and Co., 1902.

This manual of ironwork focuses on light strap
iron which can be formed cold into a variety of
products. It contains descriptions of the tools
and techniques necessary to form leaves, flowers,
scrolls, and sconces into lamps, frames, screens,
grills, stands, and candlesticks. The emphasis is
on rivets and collars to hold work together rather
than welding. It thoroughly explores scrollwork,
offering many suggestions for designs in traditional blacksmithing. Also of value are the construction details of the various pieces which can
easily be applied to forge work. 160 pp., ill.,
ind.

Hasluck, Paul N. Metalworking: A Book of Tools,
Materials, and Processes for the Handyman. Philadelphia: David McKay, Publisher, 1907.

This is a voluminous treatise on a variety of
subjects within the metalworking field. Subjects
vary from foundry work to building a microscope.
The sections on smith's work and forging iron and
steel are considered here.

"Smith's Work" (pp. 41-97), surveys a variety of
products of the forge with emphasis on the ornamental components of implements and architectural
executions. A variety of chisel patterns, twists,
collars, scrolls, and foliated and floral ornaments are presented, including a basket handle,
water and acanthus leaves, and various rosettes.
The next section deals with some of the tools and
equipment of the ornamental smithy, including a

sheet-metal pattern for a homemade forge and illustrations of a simple bellows, followed by various
power-hammer dies for punching holes in bar stock.
The final section covers the construction of architectural pieces, beginning with historical examples
from Europe with notes on their details. Next covered are the construction of rails, fireplace
screens and fenders, various stands, andirons, and
fire tools. The material is brief but interesting
and informative, and is of use to the practicing
smith.

"Forging Iron and Steel" (pp. 259-76), surveys
the materials, tools, and equipment of the smithy,
followed by the operations of upsetting, bending,
punching, and ring bending, and concludes with considerations of forging iron and steel and welding
cast steel.

This section is very brief with no surprises and
consequently of little value to the practicing
smith and too brief for the student. 760 pp.,
ill., ind.

Kühn, Fritz. Stahlgestaltung: Entwurfslehre des Kunst-
schmiedens. Tübingen: Ernst Wasmuth, 1956.

This is an excellent source of ideas, even for
the smith who cannot read German. The illustrations
of tools and techniques are fairly self-explanatory.
This is really a design book in ornamental iron.
The pictures offer several variations on a theme
with photographs of Kühn's own work and detailed
sketches of the elements of each piece treated.
It is useful for the practicing smith and student
because of the photographs of Kühn's work,

but it would be far more valuable if it were translated into English. 239 pp., ill.

Meilach, Dona. <u>Decorative</u> <u>and</u> <u>Sculptural</u> <u>Ironwork</u>: <u>Tools,</u> <u>Techniques,</u> <u>Inspiration</u>. New York: Crown Publishers, 1976.

This is a collection of articles, illustrations of forged work, and blacksmithing processes by and of many recent and contemporary American blacksmiths. It discusses shop layout, tools, fuels, processes, operations, and techniques of the modern forge. It also describes the techniques of scroll forming, forge welding, animal head carving, blade forging, Damascus steel making, and more. It includes the work of some of the best smiths in America, in excellent black and white and color photographs, and so is of importance to the student and practicing smith. 312 pp., ill., bibliog., ind.

<u>See</u> <u>also</u>: Cross, John Alfred. <u>Metal</u> <u>Forging</u> <u>and</u> <u>Wrought</u> <u>Ironwork</u>.

Googerty, Thomas Francis. <u>Hand-Forging</u> <u>and</u> <u>Wrought-Iron</u> <u>Ornamental</u> <u>Work</u>.

Krom, Edward F. <u>Hand-Wrought</u> <u>Ironwork</u>.

Lukowitz, Joseph J. <u>Interesting</u> <u>Art-Metal</u> <u>Work</u>.

Schwartzkopf, Ernst. <u>Plain</u> <u>and</u> <u>Ornamental</u> <u>Forging</u>.

Underwood, Austin. <u>Creative</u> <u>Wrought</u> <u>Ironwork</u>.

7. Bladesmithing

Very little has been written specifically about the forging of knives and swords, probably because beyond a few suggestions and guidelines there is not much to impart except through experience. Recently there has been a great resurgence in the art of knife grinding, and several books have been written addressing that audience. Those books have a place in the smithy to the extent that the processes of finishing a blade, heat treating it, and putting a handle on it are very similar, whether the original metal was forged or ground to shape.

Abels, Robert. <u>Bowie</u> <u>Knives</u>. New York: N.p., n.d.

This pamphlet contains photographs with descriptions of ninety-one bowie knives. The descriptions cover handle materials, guard materials, dimensions, and date and place of manufacture when known. The booklet also contains photographs of eight Indian pipe tomahawks. 48 pp., ill.

Robert Abels, 157 East 64th St., New York, NY, 10021.

Barney, Richard W., and Loveless, Robert W. How to Make Knives. North Hollywood, Calif.: Beinfeld Publishing Co., 1977.

This book of knife making and finishing techniques uses a variety of processes and was written by several professional knifemakers. It contains photographs and instructions for making knives by the power-tool stock removal, hand-tool stock removal, and hand forging methods. Several handle types are discussed and the operations of polishing, heat treating, silver soldering, and sheath making are considered.

The book contains many short cuts and helpful hints in all aspects of knife making. 182 pp., ill.

Boye, David. Step-by-Step Knifemaking: You Can Do It! Emmaus, Pa.: Rodale Press, 1977.

These clear and detailed instructions on knife grinding and finishing were written for the beginner using inexpensive and uncomplicated equipment, processes, and materials to produce a sophisticated product. Using recycled materials and shop-adapted equipment, the author explains with photographs and line drawings how to make and finish the blade, handle, and sheath of the knife. He includes heat treatment, finishes, location of supplies, and an excellent and unique section on acid etching of designs into the blade surface. By substituting the forging process for the grinding sequence the blacksmith could apply this book to knife smithing. 271 pp., ill., ind.

Knowlton, Jay F. <u>Knives</u>: <u>How</u> <u>to</u> <u>Make</u> <u>Them</u> <u>in</u> <u>the</u>
<u>School</u> <u>Forge</u> <u>Shop</u>. Milwaukee: Bruce Publishing Co.,
1928.

This unique and informative booklet on the forging and finishing of a variety of knives is intended as a school shop class supplement. It covers over eighteen blade types, including daggers,
kitchen knives, and hunting knives, and the types
of handles and guards for each. Information is provided in such areas as steel types and grades,
forging procedure, heat treating processes, handle
design and manufacture, and the finishing processes of filing, grinding, and buffing.

This is a well-arranged and written manual of
knife forging through all stages; it is useful to
the smith for the variety of aspects presented in
this seldom written-about subject. 38 pp., ill.

Peterson, Harold L. <u>American</u> <u>Knives</u>: <u>The</u> <u>First</u> <u>History</u>
<u>and</u> <u>Collectors'</u> <u>Guide</u>. New York: Charles Scribner's
Sons, 1958.

This history of the types and uses of knives in
American history contains photographs and background text on bowie knives, army knives, naval
dirks, Indian knives, pocket knives, and the European knives of the first explorers and colonists.
It also contains a chapter on the manufacture and
sharpening of knives.

While overwhelmingly restricted to defensive
knives rather than domestic or trade knives, the
examples are classic and a suitable reference of
period pieces in American history. 178 pp., ill.,
ind.

Strung, Norman. An Encyclopedia of Knives. New York:
J. B. Lippincott Co., 1976.

This survey of most of the knives used in the
West today describes the shape and use of various
hunting, fishing, camping, defensive, throwing,
kitchen, and specialty knives. It includes diagrams of folding knives and one-piece knives, and
identifies their key parts. There is a very good
section on knife care and sharpening. It is useful
to the bladesmith as a reference for standard
knife shapes and uses. 219 pp., ill., ind.

8. Pattern Welded Steel

Pattern welding steel is the act of combining different alloys of steel into many layered bars through forge welding, then physically distorting these layers before finishing the item to reveal the created pattern.

This ancient process was brought to perfection in many unrelated parts of the ancient world, answering a common need to produce a strong blade from unpredictable materials. The relatively difficult technique of physically combining iron and steel into a plywood type of structural relationship was developed into what is perhaps the most profound display of the blacksmith's art, the pattern welded blade. So little has been written on the subject to aid the present-day blacksmith in continuing the art that all relevant material has been listed here, including magazine articles and appendexes in books.

Chikashige, Masumi. Alchemy and Other Chemical
Achievements of the Ancient Orient: The Civilization
of Japan and China in Early Times as Seen from the
Chemical Point of View. Tokyo: Rokakuho Uchida, 1936.

   The final chapter contains a look at the methods
   of manufacturing Japanese swords by folding and
   forge welding. The processes of forging are based
   on known techniques and the metallurgical examination of swords from different periods. 103 pp.,
   ill.

Davidson, Hilda Roderick Ellis. The Sword in Anglo-
Saxon England: Its Archaeology and Literature. Oxford,
England: Clarendon Press, 1962.

   Of particular interest to Damascus steel aficio-
   nados is a report in Appendix A (pp. 217-24),
   which consists of five experiments in producing
   pattern welded steels of varying complexity in an
   attempt to reproduce the patterns found in some
   ancient blades. The tools, processes, and considerations are presented, leading to conclusions as
   to what procedures were probably used in the originals and which ones were definitely not. A valuable contribution in this area.

Grancsay, Stephen V. "A Viking Chieftain's Sword."
The Metropolitan Museum of Art Bulletin 17:173-81.

   This article describes a pattern-welded sword of
   the ninth or tenth century. Background information
   includes a discussion of the development of the
   iron and steel sword since the Bronze Age and a
   description of the process of forging a pattern
   welded blade. Ill.

Greener, William Wellington. <u>The</u> <u>Gun</u> <u>and</u> <u>its</u> <u>Develop</u>-<u>ment</u>. New York: Bonanza Books, 1910.

Chapter 10, "Modern Methods of Gun Making: The Manufacture of Iron for Gun Barrels," offers a detailed description of the process of making pattern welded gun barrels from iron and steel. Beginning with the selection of steel and the puddling of iron and preparation of those materials for initial welding, the author describes in great detail the method of weldment stacking to obtain various visual effects in the finished piece, the use of special tools to form the barrel, and the process of welding. The inherent qualities and faults of many of the various methods practiced in England and Europe are compared.

The material covered offers a unusual look into the process of making Damascus gun barrels, and being rich in details, it is also applicable to making pattern welded steel generally. Pp. 229-42, ill.

Hawley, W. M. <u>Introduction</u> <u>to</u> <u>Japanese</u> <u>Swords</u>. Hollywood, Calif.: 1973.

This pamphlet is a condensed handbook of physical characteristics of Japanese swords to aid in their identification. It discusses the making of the steels used and their application in the construction of a sword. The steps in fabrication are outlined with some details provided. 19 pp., ill.

Piaskowski, J. "The Manufacture of Mediaeval Dama-
scened Knives." Journal of the Iron and Steel Institute (July 1964):561-68.

This article metallurgically examines sections
of relic blades to determine the most probable
method of manufacture, which is then supported by
references in the literature describing various
methods of pattern welding iron and steel. The
article is well researched and provides many specific procedures and formulas for making and finishing Damascus steel pattern welded blades. Pp.
561-68, ill., bibliog.

Pleiner, Radomir. Alteuropaisches Schmiedehandwerk:
Stand der Metallkundlichen Forschung. Prague: Nakla-
datelstvi Ceskoslovenske Akademie Ved, 1962.

This is a detailed study of early tools and weapons, their characteristics and manufacture. The
text is in Czechoslovakian, but the fifty illustrations are informative. Of special importance
are the reconstructions of the steps in forging
pattern welded blades and in making various farm
implements with steeled edges. This work is unusual in that the construction techniques employed
were surmised from the partially destructive processes of metallurgical examination of museum-
quality specimens. Ill.

Rawson, Philip S. The Indian Sword. Copenhagen:
Danish Arms and Armour Society, 1967.

This work contains a brief section describing
Persian Damascus blades according to pattern type
and method of manufacture. Pp. 37-39, 183, ill.,
bibliog.

Robinson, Basil William. The Arts of the Japanese
Sword. Rutland, Vt.: Charles E. Tuttle Co., 1961.

This is primarily a handbook on identification
of Japanese swords intended for the collector. Of
interest to the smith is one brief section (pp.
25-27) which discusses the making of the blade.
Too abbreviated to give more than a general view
of the process, it does contain one or two point-
ers not found in other sources. 110 pp., 100 pls.,
various other ills., ind.

Smith, Cyril Stanley. A History of Metallography: The
Development of Ideas on the Structure of Metals Before
1890. Chicago: University of Chicago Press, 1960.

This voluminous and definitive treatise on metallurgy and iron working from earliest times through
1890 concentrates on pattern welding of iron and
steel. Of particular interest to blacksmiths are
sections on Damascus blades, Damascus gun barrels,
Japanese swords, and metal etching techniques.
Other topics covered include philosophic and
scientific investigations into metallography
through crystalography, etching, chemistry, and
physics. The research into Damascus steel is most
thorough, encompassing almost every writing on the
subject. 291 pp., ill., bibliog., ind.

Wilkenson, H. "On the Cause of the External Pattern,
or the Watering of Damascus Sword Blades." Journal of
the Royal Asiatic Society (London), o.s. 4(1837):187-
93.

This brief but informative essay on the production of patterned, "Damascus," steel blades from

Indian wootz or cast steel includes many details of the process.

Yumoto, John M. The Samurai Sword: A Handbook. Rutland, Vt.: Charles E. Tuttle Co., 1958.

This general introduction to the Samurai sword covers history, types, development, and appraisal. It includes a very good series of photographs of the process used in forging a blade from different types of steels. This section omits specifics of formulas for fluxes, clay slips, and so on, but is a good general view of the process. 191 pp., ill., ind.

9. Farm Blacksmithing

Farm blacksmithing books answered the ironwork needs of the ranch and farm. These books usually concentrate on simple projects which assume very little foreknowledge of blacksmithing. Most contain sections on farriery, wagon-tire setting, and plowshare sharpening.

Bjørlykke, Per. Yrkeslaere for Smeder. Oslo: P. M. Bye and Co., 1949.

This basic blacksmithing manual covers tools, equipment, basic operations, and power hammer work. Projects include wagon wheels, cart ironing, plowshare work, staples, tongs, and a hammer head. The book is sparingly illustrated, and requires a knowledge of the language to be useful to the smith or student. 288 pp., ill., in Norwegian.

Drew, James Meddick. Blacksmithing. Saint Paul: Webb Publishing Co., 1935.

This short book discusses many aspects of smithing for the farm. Beginning with an explanation of the materials, it goes on to cover shop layout, tools, equipment, and the fire. A few basic forging operations are then covered one by one, including scarfing, welding, punching, upsetting, and riveting. Simple projects which employ the explained operations follow, including a poker, hooks, welding chain, and welding iron to steel.

The next section discusses heat treatment and includes the making of chisels, drills, knives, tongs, and a hammer. Once very helpful to the farm or ranch, this book offers one of the few treatments available today of plowshare work, setting wagon tires, and horseshoeing. This book would be useful to the contemporary smith as a reference if the need for these obscure techniques should arise. 109 pp., ill., tables. Reprinted by the Shorey Bookstore, Seattle, 1975.

Drew, James Meddick. Farm Blacksmithing. Saint Paul: Webb Publishing Co., 1901.

This brief treatment of farm blacksmithing seems to assume a certain familiarity with the tools, equipment, and operations of the smithy. The book consists of a series of projects and some supplemental discussion of nonblacksmithing topics. Beginning with a gate hook, staple, clevis pin, chain, rings, a chain hook, and bolts, the projects then undertake welding, tong making, and finally whiffletree irons. A discussion of heat treatment is followed by chisel making and plowshare sharpening. The additional topics of rope splicing and saw sharpening conclude the text. This work contains the basic essentials of farm blacksmithing with the exception of wagon tire

work, but seems too brief for the novice and too
shallow for the student. 99 pp., ill.

Friese, John Frank. Farm Blacksmithing: A Textbook
and Problem Book for Students in Agricultural Schools
and Colleges, Technical Schools, and for Farmers.
Peoria: Manual Arts Press, 1921.

It begins with a brief explanation of the tools,
equipment, and the forge fire. The majority of the
book consists of a series of graduated projects
interspaced with various technical explanations
where needed. The book includes such projects as
staples, hooks, hinges, welded chain, wrenches,
chisels, tongs, and hoof parers, presented with
dimensioned drawings and step-by-step notation.
Finally, it covers heat treatment very briefly.
Notably absent in this book are sections on plowshare work, wagon tire setting, and horseshoeing.
A very beginning text for the novice or student,
it is useful for setting up introductory demon-
strations or workshops. 92 pp., ill., ind.

Holmstrom, John Gustav. Standard Blacksmithing, Horseshoeing, and Wagon Making. Saint Paul: Webb Publishing Co., 1907.

This manual of practical blacksmithing was intended as a reference book for the practical rural
smith. The first section is a series of lessons
including anvil posture, striking, shop equipment,
the materials, and definitions of some heat treatment terms. Information on welding, the making of

anvil tools and tongs, a section on wagon tires, one on plowshares, and a section on axles follow. The remainder of the book deals with horse anatomy and corrective shoeing. Over all the book is poorly written and disjointed. Certainly careful study would reveal useful information for the practicing smith, but this book is recommended only as a reference work. 211 pp., ill., ind.

Jarvis, Reynold F., and Abbott, Cornelius. Black-smithing on the Farm. Indianapolis: Industrial Book and Equipment Co., 1925.

This practical manual for small farm shops of the 1920s was intended to give the farmer the ability to repair equipment and make tools and hardware. It begins with a discussion of the materials, tools and equipment, and fire building. Next, operations such as drawing out, bending, upsetting, welding, and heat treatment are discussed. This information is brief but to the point and well written.

The next section of the book covers basic jobs on the farm, including hay hooks, staples, hinges, hitching rings, a neck yoke center iron, and clevis pins. A good section on forging a horseshoe with crude but understandable drawings of the important steps is followed by a discussion of the anatomy of the horse's foot and corrective shoeing.

The book is completed with chapters on setting tires and sharpening plowshares.

This is a well thought-out book of practical information useful to the student and smith for its unusual projects. 81 pp., ill., ind.

Jones, Mack M. Shopwork on the Farm. New York: McGraw Hill Book Co., 1945.

This book is a general information book for many operations around the house and farm, containing only one chapter on blacksmithing. The tools and equipment are very briefly discussed followed by fire building and stock heating. The operations of cutting, bending, punching, and twisting are applied to bending eyes and a hoisting hook. A section on working and heat treating tool steel is followed by a section on forge welding including chain links. Though insufficient in itself to teach a novice, the material could be used to supplement a course or workshop. 486 pp., ill., ind.

See also: Jones, Lynn Charles. Forging and Smithing.

10. Wheelwrighting

Cart and wagon building combine the best skills of the blacksmith and the carpenter. In winter, when farmers' demands on the smithy were lowest, the manufacture of wagons and carts was undertaken by the smith in anticipation of spring demands.

Carriage building, requiring the additional skills of trimming, upholstering, and painting, was often the job of a team of specialists working in shops set up specifically for that purpose, usually in the city, where the market was larger.

Bailey, Josclyn. The Village Wheelwright and Carpenter. Shire Album 11. Aylesbury, Bucks, U. K.: Shire Publications, 1975.

This pamphlet is a short survey of the tools and operations of wagon and cart building. It contains photographs of the sawyers, the tools of wagon building, and the making of a wheel. Although brief, it is well written and informative. It would be useful as a supplement to a less profusely illustrated carriage building manual. 33 pp., ill.

Great Britain, War Office. Handbook for Carpenters, Wheelwrights, and Smiths. London: His Majesty's Stationery Office, 1934.

This detailed and thorough manual of the skills required in wagon building was written as a guide for workmen and contains many often overlooked aspects of the processes.

The first three parts deal with the carpentry aspects of wagon building. Wood is covered, from its selection as a timber, through sawing, seasoning, and preserving. The tools of the carpenter are covered in the second section, which includes instructions for sharpening and caring for saws and chisels. The third part covers the making of wooden joints and the use of fastenings and hardware.

Part 4 covers the making of wheels from design and selection of materials to fitting the pieces and repairing broken or worn-out wheels.

The last five chapters deal with the ironwork of wagons. The materials, steel and iron, are discussed, followed by a survey of the tools and equipment of the smith, including power hammers and power hammer dies. Next the smithing operations of forge welding, bolt making, collar forming, tong making, and the making of several pieces of hardware are covered as applied explicitly to wagons. An unusual section is included on making coil and leaf springs. The next part deals with drop forgings made between hollow dies and the considerations of their design and use. The last two parts deal with the heat treatment of steel,

including case hardening and carburizing, and the
metallurgy of steel and the effects of heating and
cooling.

This book is an excellent manual for the wagon
builder and wheelwright, primarily, but it is also
of value to the general blacksmith. 217 pp., ill.,
bibliog.

Lungwitz, A., and Adams, Charles F. The Complete
Guide to Blacksmithing: Horseshoeing, Carriage and
Wagon Building and Painting. Chicago: M. A. Donohue
and Co., 1902.

This basic blacksmithing manual was intended to
be used in rural shops. The first part offers 40
pages of general blacksmithing, including a description of the basic equipment and tools and
brief descriptions of the basic operations of
smithing with discussions of forge welding and
case hardening. No examples or projects are presented, and the treatment is very brief.

The second part deals at length with farriery,
including horse anatomy, basic shoeing, and corrective shoeing. This section would probably be
useful to farriers.

The last part covers various aspects of carriage
and wagon building, including ironing, wheel ironing and building, tire setting, carpentry work,
and painting and finishing. The information in
this last part, particularly on ironing, is unique,
as each major component of the assembly is described and the forging discussed. Unfortunately
there are no illustrations in this section, and
the brief descriptions are useful only to someone

already in the business of building or restoring carriages and wagons.

Over all the book has many helpful hints and useful information, but is poorly illustrated, and the text is sometimes hard to follow. It would be especially useful to the wheelwright and wagon builder. 222 pp., ill.

Phillipson, John. The Art and Craft of Coachbuilding. Technological Handbooks. London: George Bell and Sons, 1897.

This book of practical carriage building discusses the many aspects of the trade. It contains chapters on preparation for coach building, including design, engineering considerations, and the selection of woods. These are followed by chapters on the actual construction of the frame, carriage, wheels, and ironwork. The finishing steps of painting and trimming conclude the text. This book would be useful to the wagon or carriage builder for the tools and design considerations as well as for many elements of construction. 197 pp., ill., tables, ind.

Reist, Arthur L. Conestoga Wagon: Masterpiece of the Blacksmith. Lancaster, Pa.: Forry and Hacker, 1975.

This is a well-researched book of lore about the Conestoga wagon, its evolution, use, construction, and cultural significance. It illustrates in photographs and drawings much of the iron hardware employed in a typical "Prairie Schooner." The next concentrates on the Conestoga wagon's importance to its culture as presented in records, accounts, stories, and pictures from the period of use. The

booklet does not discuss how the wagon was built
nor the forging of the iron. 50 pp., ill., bibliog.

Richardson, Milton Thomas, ed. Practical Carriage
Building. New York: 1891.

This is a volume of excerpts from "Blacksmith
and Wheelwright" magazine that covers many aspects
of carriage and coach building. It deals with isolated procedures, often with an improved idea or
solution to a particular problem. It covers many
wheel-making processes not found elsewhere. It
would be valuable to the coach builder and wheelwright as a reference book but not as a manual because the approach to the subject is rather disjointed. 222 pp., ill., ind.

Sturt, George [bourne]. The Wheelwright's Shop.
London: Cambridge University Press, 1923.

This autobiography of the owner of a late nineteenth-century English wheelwright shop was written after the decline in the industry to record
the complexity of the various trades in the once
essential production of wagons and carts.

Every trade that played a part is considered,
including the sawyers, blacksmiths, carpenters,
and wheelwrights. A great deal of attention is
given to the particular components of the wagon or
cart, including the parts of the vehicles and
their structural considerations, the care in selection of materials, the execution of jobs, some of
the problems encountered, and the skills required
to solve them. The book gives a very detailed picture of the workings of a large interrelated shop
and also provides an understanding of the industry.

While it was not intended to provide working knowledge of the processes, the book does consider many
practical details and would be of value especially
if used with a more technical carriage building
manual. 235 pp., ill., ind.

See also: Richardson, M. T. <u>Practical Blacksmithing</u>.

Drew, James Meddick. <u>Farm Blacksmithing</u>.

Jarvis, Reynold F. <u>Blacksmithing on the Farm</u>.

11. Industrial Forging

Industrial forging books focus on topics which are generally beyond the scope of the small smithy. Some of the books describe the forge work of specific industries, such as shipbuilding or locomotive construction. Many of the books deal more generally with large shop operations, including general layout, forging machinery, and production heat treatment equipment. The projects describe massive forgings and some tool making, often emphasizing the use of the power hammer.

Alabama State Department of Education. "Blacksmithing for the Shipyard: Suggested Training Course in Blacksmithing for the Shipyard." Mimeographed. Mobile, 1941.

This book is intended to guide blacksmiths of ship fittings and components in the selection of materials and the processes of forging various jobs.

The book begins with general information, including identification of steel, testing for hardness, judging temper colors, furnaces and fuels,

heat treatment, and a list of tools and equipment.
General jobs are then covered, including fire
building, hardening and tempering edge tools, and
case hardening.

A section on bending jobs is followed by a section on forging jobs, such as a spud bar, hatch
cover dog, horn cleat, cold chisel, hot chisel,
socket wrench, and a drop bolt.

The final section covers welding in such jobs as
a pull bolt and an anchor windlass brake band.

While most of the projects in this book are
specialized to the ship-building industry, the
principles set forth in those jobs are applicable
to general smith work. Some of the projects are
useful in nonindustrial applications, including
the material on the power hammer and its tools.
This book would be useful to the smith and student
for supplemental information on principles and
tool applications. Unpaginated, ill.

Cran, James. _Blacksmith Shop Practice_. Machinery's
Reference Series no. 61. New York: The Industrial
Press, 1910.

These articles on several topics related to the
industrial shop were taken from _Machinery_ magazine.
The first article concerns the layout of an industrial shop, including relative locations of the
tool racks, forges, anvils, and blowers, considerations of foundations, walls and flooring, and the
positioning of offices, lockers, and wash rooms.

The second article discusses forge welding of
large pieces, including the use of cranes and a

portable forge for moving the heat to the bar
rather than the bar to the forge.

The third article discusses the forging of hooks
and chains and the considerations of materials and
tools used.

The last article covers several different topics
and projects, including making a homemade forge,
drawing out tool steel under the power hammer,
forging eye bolts from the solid, and punching
collars under the power hammer.

This book offers a variety of information for
the industrial shop that is somewhat useful and
applicable to the modern smith. 40 pp., ill.

Dunaev, P. A. Kuznechnoe delo v MTM. Moscow, 1954.

This Russian industrial forging manual illustrates some tools, equipment, and operations of
the power hammer. It is of marginal usefulness to
the English-speaking smith, since only a few of
the pictures are self-explanatory and a source of
ideas. 128 pp., ill.

Horner, Joseph Gregory. Smithing and Forging. Man-
chester, U. K.: Emmott and Co., 1920.

This treatise was prepared for the use of shops
utilizing presses, furnaces, and power hammers in
the production of large forgings such as locomotive axles, levers, and crankshafts.

A section on industrial shop layout, including
the installation of power hammers, is followed by
a description of hand tools and hand operations,
with examples of some industrial forgings made at
the anvil. A large section covers examples of
stamped work, forms of dies, drop hammer work

using those dies, and forging and upsetting machine
work. A survey of heating furnaces and the heat
treatment of large forgings concludes the book.

The book contains knowledge usable by the practicing smith, particularly in the areas of machine
set-up, furnaces, and heat treatment. The use of
special closed dies, the main emphasis of the book,
limits its usefulness for the small smithy. 222
pp., ill., ind.

Johnson, Carl Gunnard. Forging Practice: A Practical
Treatise on Hand Forging of Wrought Iron, Machine
Steel, and Tool Steel; Drop Forging; and Heat Treat-
ment of Steel, Including Annealing, Hardening, and
Tempering. Chicago: American Technical Society, 1938.

This industrial forging treatise is intended to
familiarize the reader with various processes and
equipment used in mass forgings of steel.

Background information includes brief discussions of the hand-forge tools and operations, and
power-hammer tools and operations.

Brief discussions follow on various processes,
including drop forging, bulldozer upsetting
machines, hydraulic forging, cold and hot rolling,
cold swaging, pressing and drawing out, extrusion,
and spinning.

Supplemental information on defects in forgings,
heat treatment, and identification of steel completes the book.

This book is valuable for the smith in metallurgy
and power-hammer tooling. 136 pp., ill., bibliog.,
ind.

Kamenshchikov, G. <u>Forging</u> <u>Practice</u>. Moscow: Foreign
Language Publishing House, 1960.

This is a voluminous treatise of modern industrial forgework from hand tools to hydraulic
presses as applied to machine building.

The introductory materials and equipment chapters include bench operations such as chiseling,
filing, and drilling; the qualities and grades of
steels; various furnaces, including design, construction, and operation; and the various factors
affecting the heating of steel, including grain
size changes and the effects of overheating.

A chapter on hand forging includes the tools for
the operations of drawing out, upsetting, bending,
punching, and forge welding, and is followed by
examples of uses, including bolts and a socket
wrench.

The book then deals with the special problems
and applications of machine forging. This section
begins with a chapter on the effects of forging,
stock calculations and selection of stock. Next is
a chapter on power hammers of several types, and a
chapter on power-hammer tools with applications of
those tools in examples.

There follow several chapters on presses, auto-
matic forging and stamping machines, and drop
forging, all covered in depth as to selection,
use, and special considerations of each.

A chapter on forging nonferrous metals, carbon
and alloy steels, is followed by chapters on heat
treatment and inspection, organization of the shop,
and a final chapter on safety engineering.

The book is clearly written, detailed and simple enough to understand and apply. It is of value to any smith employing power forging equipment or building heat-treatment furnaces. 483 pp., ill., tables.

Labor and Industry, Department of. Industrial Blacksmithing. New South Wales, Australia: 1969.

This pamphlet is a survey of the job market possibilities of industrial smithing written to encourage young people to enter the field. It discusses the various jobs involved, skills required, and personality traits needed to become a smith. 9 pp.

Miller, Joseph K. Machine Forging, Parts 1 and 2. Scranton, Pa.: International Textbook Co., 1936.

This two-part book was written for International Correspondence Schools on the power hammer and power press and the applications of each.

Part 1 deals with various power hammers from small to large and the advantages and applications of each. Types covered include the helve, board, steam, eccentric, and drop hammers. Examples of operations include both closed and open die, as well as hand-held tool, forgings. Projects include a connecting rod, a crankshaft, forging high carbon steel, and forge welding.

Part 2 covers the less-used machines of the industrial shop and their applications, including hydraulic and steam presses, a rivet-making machine, a universal forging machine, hot sawing and burring machines, a thread rolling and a graded rolling machine. Examples and projects are absent, the emphasis being on the working principles of a broad range of machines rather than on how to use a particular type.

The book contains information on a variety of unusual forging machines which could find their way into a modern smithy and therefore it is useful as a reference book for the smith. 132 pp., ill.

Naujoks, Waldemar, and Fabel, Donald C. Forging Handbook. Cleveland: The American Society for Metals, 1936.

This voluminous treatise on most aspects of industrial forging, presented in detail, was intended as a reference within the forging industry.

It contains background information on the history of forging, including a survey of the earliest power hammers. It also contains sections on equipment, die block making, forge tools, various forging machines, effects of forging, finishing, cleaning, testing, and heat treatment of forgings.

Supplemental information on materials handling, plant maintenance, furnace design, product design, materials selection, job estimating, and shop safety conclude the volume.

Except for sections on steel selection, metallurgy, and the tables, this is of limited use to the practicing smith, owing to the scale of the machines and processes. 644 pp., ill., tables, ind.

Rusinoff, Samuel Eugene. _Forging_ _and_ _Forming_ _Metals_.
Chicago: American Technical Society, 1952.

This text on industrial forging machines and
practices is intended to prepare the student for
industry.

It begins with background information on the
history of forging, considerations of advantages
of forging, a survey of hand forging, and basic
power-hammer forging for the small blacksmith shop.

Sections on industrial forging practices of
closed and open die drop forging, press and upset
forging are followed by techniques of cleaning,
heat treating, and inspection of products. A chapter on making closed dies is followed by sections
on product design, safety, and tolerances.

This book is only marginally useful to the nonindustrial shop. There is some good information on
the power hammer and its tools though, which would
be useful to the smith. 279 pp., ill., tables,
bibliog., ind.

Science of Railways Cyclopedia. _Smith_ _Shop_ _Practice:_
_A_ _Practical_ _Textbook_ _for_ _the_ _Instruction_ _of_ _Black-_
smiths, _their_ _Helpers,_ _and_ _Apprentices_ _in_ _Railway_
Employ, _and_ _Others_ _Interested_ _in_ _the_ _Operation_ _of_
Forge _and_ _Foundry_ _Equipment_. Chicago: Railway Train-
ing Institute, 1926.

This is an extensive treatise on many aspects of
iron and steel forging, particularly as it relates
to the railroad industry.

The book begins with a section on shop smith
tools and an extensive survey of various types of
Buffalo Forge Co. equipment, followed by a survey

of power hammers and forging machines. A discussion follows on the history of iron and steel development, including a chronology of important advances in the art. The next several chapters deal with basic blacksmithing, including materials, heating, basic hand forging operations, fire welding, heat treatment, and tool forging. A chapter on the steam hammer contains examples of some applications, such as tongs, chisels and the use of tools.

A section titled "Blacksmith Shop Kinks" covers a wide range of problems, techniques, and processes in the manufacture of various locomotive forgings. A section on forging machine dies is followed by two sections on foundry practices and castings.

This book is valuable to the practicing smith for its detailed treatment of a variety of material relevant to the smithy. 446 pp., ill., tables, ind.

Part Three

Historical Background of the Profession

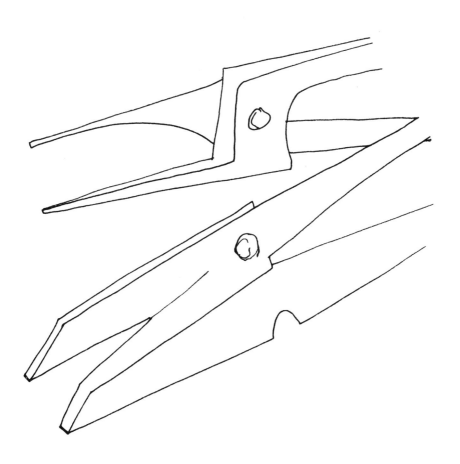

12. Historical Background of the Profession

This chapter presents a potpourri of nontechnical books dealing with various aspects of blacksmithing. Included here are books on the mythology, lore, and early written references to blacksmithing; descriptions of the smith and smithy in a nostalgic vein; historical studies of specific periods, such as Colonial American smithing; and books on the processes, tools, and products of the forge written for a general readership and too simplified to be of much use even to the student smith.

Bailey, Josclyn. The Village Blacksmith. Shire Album 24. Aylesbury, Bucks, U. K.: Shire Publications, 1977.

This is a brief vignette of the blacksmith and some of the processes of the shop in the late nineteenth century. It describes the tools, equipment, operations, and processes generally used. Photographs and descriptive captions for setting a wagon tire rim, making a horseshoe, and making an ornamental poker handle are given. Too brief to be of much value for learning blacksmithing, this work is more of a general overview of the types of

things blacksmiths did and would therefore appeal
more to a general audience than to the student or
smith. 33 pp., ill., bibliog.

Christian, Marcus Bruce. Negro Ironworkers in Louisiana, 1718-1900. Gretna, LA.: Pelican Publishing Co.,
1972.

This is a scholarly essay on the part blacks
played in the making of ironwork in Louisiana, and
in New Orleans in particular. The important part
the black played as blacksmith is scantily recorded
and only indirectly documented, primarily owing to
his status as a slave during the greater part of
the period studied. The existence of black smiths
is supported by various factors, including the
native skill of smithing which they brought with
them from Africa, and the high price slaves trained
in smithing brought at the auction block.

The influence of black ironworkers was considerable throughout the development of the area, until
the increased use of casting, mass production, and
the general phasing out of blacksmithing effected
its gradual decline, around 1900. 61 pp., ill.

Clarke, Mary Stetson. Pioneer Ironworks. New York:
Chilton Book Co., 1968.

This is a general audience book about the found-
ing and developing of the Saugus Iron Works in
Saugus, Massachusetts, its people and its products.
The operations of making charcoal, refining iron
ore, and manufacturing iron are described. The re-
finement of iron by forging, rolling, and splitting on various water-powered devices is explained
and illustrated in detail. Besides its value as a

history of the area, the descriptions of water-
powered machinery are useful to anyone construct-
ing such a facility. 81 pp., ill.

Dunshee, Kenneth Holcomb. The Village Blacksmith.
Early American Occupations Series. Watkins Glen,
N. Y.: Century House, 1957.

This pamphlet is a profile of the American blacksmith, primarily in his role as farrier, from
Colonial days to the present. It contains descriptions of the tools, operations, and equipment of
the smith and the farrier. Many illustrations are
taken from archives, museums, and present-day
shops. It is a nostalgic work that is too brief to
be of much use to the practicing smith. 48 pp.,
ill.

Fisher, Leonard Everett. The Blacksmiths. Colonial
American Craftsmen series. New York: Franklin Watts,
1976.

This history of Colonial iron working is intended
for a general readership. It briefly discusses the
original development of the industry in America,
including the role Great Britain played, and the
need for smiths in the New World. It covers the
manufacture of several common products, including
nails, axes, and horseshoes. It is a very brief
introduction to this period of American blacksmithing. 47 pp., ill., ind.

Gill, Harold B., Jr. The Blacksmith in Eighteenth-
Century Williamsburg: An Account of his Life and
Times and of His Craft. Williamsburg Craft Series.
Edited by Thomas K. Ford. Williamsburg, Va.: Colonial
Willaimsburg, 1971.

This brief treatise on the earliest blacksmiths
of the American colonies is intended for the historian. It discusses the development of iron manufacture, the growth of the smithing trades, and
their effect on commerce and the prosperity of the
era. Definitions are presented of some of the
equipment, tools, and processes employed. The
pamphlet concludes with biographies of several
Williamsburg blacksmiths.

This study is an interesting insight into the
role that this very essential element of civilization played in the lives of the early settlers and
in the political relationship with Great Britain
immediately prior to the Revolution. 30 pp., ill.,
bibliog.

Hazen, Edward. Popular Professions: Or, Professions
and Trades. Vol. 2. New York: Harper and Brothers,
1841.

This series of vignettes of various professions
and trades is often accompanied by an engraving of
a typical shop scene which describes the product
and, to a lesser extent, the processes used. Of
interest to the smith are the trades of iron and
steel making, blacksmithing, nail making, cutlery
making, and gunsmithing. The volume contains interesting and sometimes useful information. 275
pp., ill.

Hibben, Thomas. The Sons of Vulcan: The Story of
Metals. Philadelphia: J. B. Lippincott Co., 1940.

This is a history of metalworking throughout the
world. The extraction and working of gold, copper,
bronze, and iron in ancient times is followed
through the centuries with the development of improved technologies in extraction, furnace designs,
improved fuels, and metallurgical knowledge. The
book surveys the early uses of iron, including the
tools, weapons, and implements, with their techniques of construction. The author connects the
use of improved iron- and steel-making facilities
to the industrial era and the steam engine. The
book also contains a survey of wagons, carriages,
and carts, and the making of rivets, axes, and
weapons. One chapter surveys the tools and processes of the blacksmith. 259 pp., ill.

Hogg, Gary. Hammer and Tongs: Blacksmithery Down the
Ages. London: Hutchinson and Co., 1964.

This is a historical survey of blacksmithing in
England over the past several centuries. This book
begins with the earliest historical references to
blacksmithing in mythology and continues with a
description of the forge, its tools and equipment.
Sections follow on making a horseshoe and shoeing
the horse. Ornamental iron development is followed
by a discussion of some ornamental techniques and
an essay on the hanging of a gate taken from
Stevenson's The Din of a Smithy.

This book is intended for general readership and
offers little in the way of technical information
for the smith. 159 pp., ill., ind.

Kauffman, Henry J. <u>Early</u> <u>American</u> <u>Ironware:</u> <u>Cast</u> <u>and</u>
<u>Wrought</u>. Rutland, Vt.: Charles Tuttle Co., 1966.

 This is a general survey of the various metal
working trades, including the blacksmith, founder,
farrier, locksmith, gunsmith, nailer, wheelwright,
and the tinsmith. Each area is briefly discussed
and a few examples of the products are presented.
It contains some interesting historical points and
useful designs of pieces. 166 pp., ill.

Knauth, Percy. <u>The</u> <u>Metalsmiths</u>. The Emergence of Man
series. New York: Time-Life Books, 1974.

 This history of the metalworking industry is
intended for a general readership. It contains a
chapter on iron which discusses the origins of
iron working, and wurveys the processes developed
in its rise in importance, including lamination of
iron and steel for tools, and weapon technology.
This is an interesting but very summarized treatment of blacksmithing's origins and development.
160 pp., ill., ind.

Mateaux, C. L., and Rose, Joshua. <u>The</u> <u>Wonderland</u> <u>of</u>
<u>Work</u>. New York: Cassell and Co., 1884.

 This well-written children's book describes many
industrial processes of the late 1800s. It contains sections on steel making, power-hammer work,
blacksmithing, file cutting, pin making, knife
forging, and spoon making. It also contains detailed engravings of various power hammers, machine
tools, and hand tools. These subjects were so common in the authors' day that they received little
attention in the literature so this book gives an

unusual insight into the light industry of the late nineteenth century. 171 pp., ill.

Robbins, Frederick W. The Smith: Traditions and Lore of an Ancient Craft. London: Rider and Co., 1953.

This excellent treatise following blacksmithing through history from various sources in religion, mythology, folklore, and poetry, is arranged chronologically to show the progression of the trade from the Bronze age to the present, throughout the world.

The earliest evidence of man's forging abilities is discussed, followed by evidences of primitive iron-making furnaces. The relationship of primitive iron workers to their environment and their technical abilities is considered, along with their place in society, how they were treated and compensated for their labors.

The social role of the smith is considered in Roman and Greek mythology, in various castes and guilds, and in the position smiths occupied in the society. There are several stories and poems from European sources spanning several centuries.

This scholarly approach to the place blacksmithing has occupied throughout history, as recounted from original sources, will be of interest to the general reader and blacksmith alike. 160 pp., ill., ind.

Smith, Donald. Metalwork: An Introductory Historical Survey. London: B. T. Batsford, 1948.

This brief literary survey of types of metalwork, including chapters on the blacksmith, locksmith,

swordsmith, and the armorer, was written for
schools. The text is supplemented by twenty-two
plates. 64 pp., ill., ind.

Stevenson, J. A. R. The Din of a Smithy. London:
Chapman and Hall, 1932.

This autobiography of a young English smith
describes his development and learning process
from apprentice to owner of a five-man shop. This
book is particularly entertaining for the smith
because of the universal problems encountered and
their solutions.

The text sequentially covers and discusses the
major commissions of the author from his first
ornamental pieces to sophisticated gates. The
author includes sections on design, the materials,
and the making of a candlestick, a trivet, and a
gate. This book is full of advice on dealing with
the public, designing and pricing items, and running a smithy. This unique and often amusing insight into the workings of a small shop is of particular interest to the smith because so much of
the advice "hits home." 171 pp., ill., ind.

Watson, Aldren Auld. The Village Blacksmith. New York:
Thomas Y. Crowell Co., 1968.

This is a historical description of the smithy,
the smith, the forge tools and equipment, and many
techniques and operations used by the American
blacksmith since the Colonial period.

The text emphasizes the importance smith work
played in the community, from the extraction of
iron from its ore to the manufacture of the many
implements, tools, and hardware of the smithy.

The principle elements of the trade are illustrated and discussed, including the tools, equipment, and operations of the forge. The making of
horseshoes, wagon iron, hinges, bolts, hooks, hammers, and axes are described and illustrated.

This book has general appeal and includes ideas
and methods of manufacture which would be meaning-
ful and of value to the practicing smith. 125 pp.,
ill., ind.

Webber, Ronald. The Village Blacksmith. Newton Abbot,
Devon, England: David & Charles, 1971.

This is a popular history of the English blacksmith from Celtic times to the present. The book
discusses the organizations of blacksmiths, surveys the tools and equipment of the forge, includes
several stories and tales, and discusses the relationship of the smith to English society. The
author has included many reproductions of original
woodcuts, drawings, paintings, and engravings
depicting blacksmithing and farriery. This work
will be of interest to a general readership and,
to a lesser extent, to students and smiths interested in the historical background of the trade.
160 pp., ill., bibliog.

See also: Hawley, J. E. The Blacksmith and His Art.

Part Four

Products of the Forge

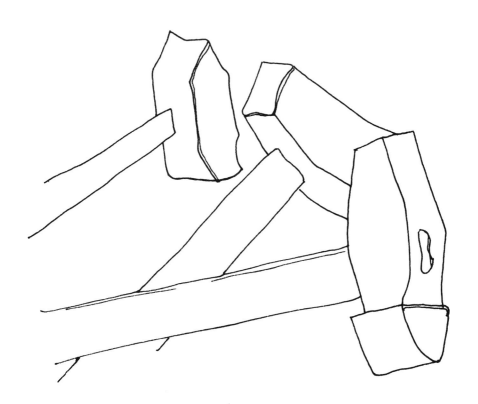

13. Lighting Fixtures

Gould, George Glen, and Gould, Florence (Holden). Period Lighting Fixtures. New York: Dodd, Mead and Co., 1928.

This is a history of the development of lighting devices throughout Europe and America over the past millennium. The examples are generally of an elaborate and ornate style and relatively few of them are of wrought iron. The photographs are few and are scattered throughout the text. 274 pp., ill., ind.

Hayward, Arthur H. Colonial and Early American Lighting. 1923. Reprint. New York: Dover Publications, 1962.

This book surveys a broad range of lighting devices of all types and materials. It contains a few examples of iron betty lamps, candle holders, candlestands, and chandeliers. The wrought iron examples, while few in number, are of excellent quality and design and are well photographed. 198 pp., ill.

Kühn, Fritz; Schindler, Ernst; and Di Michiel, M. L.
<u>Leuchten</u>: <u>Lampen, Windlichter, Laternen, Leuchter</u>.
Colemans Entwurfsmappen für das metallverarbeitende
Handwerk series, vol. 7. Lübeck: Charles Coleman,
Verlag, 1966.

This is a collection of working drawings for
contemporary German lighting devices, including
lanterns; wall, floor and hanging lamps; candelabra; and table and ceiling lamps employing forged
iron, brass, copper, and glass. 9 unnumbered pp.,
32 pls., ill., in German, French, and English.

Rushlight Club, The. <u>Early Lighting</u>: <u>A Pictorial
Guide</u>. Boston: The Rushlight Club, 1972.

This is a very complete survey of lighting
devices from prehistory to the early twentieth
century. Many examples of wrought iron are presented, including cressets, rushlights, splint
holders, candle holders, candlestands, chandeliers,
grease lamps, miners' canlesticks, and others.
This is an outstanding representation of forged
lighting devices. 129 pp., ill.

Vogt, Paul. <u>Leuchter und Lampen aus Stahl</u>. Düsseldorf:
Stahleisen, G.m.b.H., 1963.

This is a survey of iron and steel lighting devices from early grease lamps to modern electric
fixtures. It contains examples of candle holders,
candlestands, lanterns, and chandeliers of historic and modern execution in both simple and very
ornate styles. There is much information and many
ideas here for the smith. Text in German. 135 pp.,
ill.

14. Hardware and Tools

Braun-Feldwig, Wilhelm. Schmiedeeisen und Leichtmetall am Bau: Kunstschmiedeund Schlosserarbeiten. Ravensburg, Germany: Otto Maier, 1952.

This collection of contemporary German ironwork is presented through photographs of various pieces accompanied by drawings of construction details of the examples. It includes grills, gates, panels, lighting devices, stairway balustrades, sculpture, and door hardware. The text is in German with 335 illustrations which are of good quality, informative, and of use to the blacksmith. 118 pp., ill.

British Museum. A Guide to the Antiquities of the Early Iron Age of Central and Western Europe, Including the British Late-Keltic Period. Oxford: Horace Hart, 1905.

This is a detailed survey of the artifacts of the late Celtic period in Great Britain, including the earliest iron implements. It contains a few engravings and descriptions of iron swords, digging tools, jewelry, and currency bars from a period when iron was still rare and bronze occu-

pied most of the common uses. This volume is of
limited interest to the smith, as its emphasis is
strongly on materials other than iron. 158 pp.,
ill., ind.

Corbin, P., and Corbin, F. Colonial and Early English
Hardware. New Britain, Conn., 1931.

This is a catalogue of products offered by this
company presented in drawings, photographs, and
illustrations of the hardware installed. It includes hinges, door pulls, handles, door knockers,
lock and doorbell escutcheons, latches, sliding
bolts, letter boxes, foot scrapers, shutter dogs,
and sash hardware. Most of the pieces are forged
and many styles are presented as matched sets.
82 pp., ill.

D'Allemagne, Henry René. Decorative Antique Ironwork:
A Pictorial Treasury. Introduced and translated by
Vera K. Ostoia. New York: Dover Publications, 1968.

This book consists of photographs of thousands
of examples of cast, forged, and tooled ironwork
of Europe from the seventeenth, eighteenth, and
nineteenth centuries. It includes examples of
grills, locks, door hardware, signs, jewelry, cutlery, smoking accessories, furniture, lighting
fixtures, tools, instruments, and kitchen utensils.
The objects selected strongly emphasize the ornate
and embellished examples of pieces belonging to
the wealthy, rather than simple, utilitarian articles of the common classes. 415 pp., ill.

Frank, Edgar B. Old French Ironwork: The Craftsman and His Art. Cambridge, Mass.: Harvard University Press, 1950.

This scholarly treatise on antique French ironwork includes tools, locks, keys, door hardware, smoking accessories, and household utensils, presented in 446 photographs with introductory passages. Much of the work is highly elaborate and ornate and many examples in each category are presented. 221 pp., ill., ind.

Handberg, Ejner. Shop Drawings of Shaker Iron and Tinware. Stockbridge, Mass.: Berkshire Traveller Press, 1976.

This is a collection of dimensioned drawings of Shaker wrought iron, cast iron, and tinware products. The wrought iron examples include door latches and hinges, foot scrapers, fireplace tools, and kitchen utensils. Some of these items are illustrated in photographs at the end of the book. 87 pp., ill., ind.

Hankenson, Dick. Trivets, Book 1. Des Moines, Iowa: Wallace-Homestead Book Co., 1972.

This is primarily a photographic collection of cast iron laundry trivets with additional sections on tile, brass, and wire, and seven examples of wrought iron trivets. 118 pp., ill., ind.

Hankenson, Dick. Trivets: Old and Reproductions, Book 2. Des Moines: Wallace-Homestead Book Co., 1972.

This photographic collection of cast iron, brass, and wire laundry trivets includes fourteen examples of hand wrought iron trivets. 144 pp., ill., ind.

Hill, Conover. <u>Antique</u> <u>Tools</u>: <u>An</u> <u>Illustrated</u> <u>Value</u>
<u>Guide</u>. Paducah, Ky.: Schroeder Publishing Co., 1975.

This collection of early American tools is
depicted by crude line drawings and supplemented
by a relative value guide. Areas covered include
blacksmith tools, carpenters' tools, saws, farriers' tools, measuring devices, axes, farm tools,
and other general trade tools. 123 pp., ill.

Hill, Conover. <u>Early</u> <u>American</u> <u>Primitives</u>: <u>An</u> <u>Illus-</u>
<u>trated</u> <u>Value</u> <u>Guide</u>. Paducah, Ky.: Collector Books,
1975.

This collection of antique implements, utensils,
and tools of the rural household is presented in
dated line drawings accompanied by estimated cur-
rent value. Articles of interest to the blacksmith
include books, utensils, nails, assorted axes, and
tools. The illustrations do not suggest methods of
construction as the renditions are too crude.
102 pp., ill.

Horst, Melvin J., and Smith, Elmer L. <u>Early</u> <u>Iron</u> <u>Ware</u>.
Lebanon, Pa.: Applied Arts Publishers, 1971.

This is a brief collection of American cast and
wrought ironware presented in photographs with
accompanying text. Forged articles include trammels, hooks, utensils, trivets, lighting devices,
and andirons. 32 pp., ill.

Kauffman, Henry J. <u>American</u> <u>Axes</u>: <u>A</u> <u>Survey</u> <u>of</u> <u>Their</u>
<u>Development</u> <u>and</u> <u>Their</u> <u>Makers</u>. Brattleboro, Vt.:
Stephen Greene Press, 1972.

This survey of the American ax and its historical
development is presented textually with a portfolio

of examples in photographs. It follows the evolution of the ax, from early European examples,
through each century of American usage. Many different types of axes are discussed, including hew-
ing, broad, mortising, trade, and turf-cutting
types. The volume covers methods of manufacture,
advice on care and use, and a directory of ax
makers. It is of use to the blacksmith for making
accurate reproductions. 151 pp., ill.

Klamkin, Charles. Weather Vanes: The History, Design,
and Manufacture of an American Folk Art. New York:
Hawthorne Books, 1973.

This collection includes American weather vanes
of all types and description, primarily in sheet
metal, wood, and copper, with a few examples in
wrought iron. An introductory text accompanies the
profuse illustrations. Although it is intended for
collectors, it is of some use to the smith. 209
pp., ill., ind.

Kühn, Fritz; Schindler, Ernst; and Di Michiel, M. L.
Geschmiedete Werbung: Wandplastiken, Zeichen, Schrif-
ten. Colemans Entwurfsmappen für das metallverarbeitende Handwerk series, vol. 8. Lübeck: Charles Coleman,
Verlag, 1967.

This collection of contemporary German designs
of animal, plant, and human forms as applied to
commercial advertisement and signs is presented in
working drawings. 9 pp., 35 pls., in German, French,
and English.

Kühn, Fritz; Schindler, Ernst; and Di Michiel, M. L.
Gesellenstücke: Schlosser-, Schmiede-, Metallbau-
Arbeiten. Colemans Entwurfsmappen für das metallver-
arbeiten Handwerk series, vol. 3. Lübeck: Charles
Coleman, Verlag, 1965.

> This volume contains designs and working draw-
> ings of contemporary German interior ironwork,
> including fireplace accessories, grillwork, light-
> ing devices, and a variety of other pieces. 9 pp.,
> 36 pls.

Lindsay, J. Seymour. Iron and Brass Implements of the
English House. Chapters in Art series no. 39. Introduction by Ralph Edwards. London: Alec Tiranti, 1970.

> This voluminous survey of the forged articles of
> antique British manufacture is presented in line
> drawings and accompanying text. Areas covered
> include fireplace accessories, cooking utensils,
> lighting devices, smoking accoutrements, and a
> brief survey of American Colonial implements. Some
> of the articles chosen are of fairly sophisticated
> and decorated design, but many are simple, clean,
> and well-suited to study and reproduction. 88 pp.
> text, 473 ill., ind.

Neumann, George C., and Kravic, Frank J. Collector's
Illustrated Encyclopedia of the American Revolution.
Secaucus, N. J.: Castle Books, 1975.

> This is a thorough and profusely illustrated
> collection of the artifacts of the American Revo-
> lution. Of interest to the smith are sections on
> andirons, axes, trivets, blades, stirrups, nails,
> and tools from this period, all presented in photo-
> graphs. 286 pp., ill., bibliog.

Nutting, Wallace. Early American Ironwork. Saugus,
Mass.: Wallace Nutting, 1919.

This volume contains sketches and photographs,
with descriptive text, of a variety of antique
ironware, including fireplace accessories, trivets,
lighting devices, kitchen utensils, door hardware,
sash hardware, foot scrapers, and weather vanes.
The author presents a variety of clean and interesting designs. 24 pp., ill.

Nutting, Wallace. Furniture of the Pilgrim Century:
(Of American Origin) 1620-1720, with Maple and Pine
to 1800, Including Colonial Utensils and Wrought-Iron
House Hardware into the Nineteenth Century. Framing-
ton, Mass.: Old America Co., Publishers, 1921.

This voluminous treatise on furniture includes a
short subchapter on wrought iron with seven pages
of photographs of kitchen utensils, fireplace
accessories, hinges, and lighting devices.

Pennsylvania Farm Museum of Landis Valley. The Blacksmith: Artisan Within the Early Community. Foreward
by Blanch K. Reigle, introduction by John D. Tyler,
edited by Vernon S. Gunnion and Carroll J. Hopf.
Harrisburg: Pennsylvania Historical and Museum Com-
mission, 1972.

This well-illustrated pamphlet catalogs 103 objects of early American wrought ironwork from the
collection of Henry and George Landis, including
decorative hinges, hasps, utensils, hardware, and
utilitarian tools and implements. Many unusual
pieces are presented, such as Conestoga wagon
hardware and farm tools. 64 pp., ill.

Perry, Evan. Collecting Antique Metalware. Garden
City, N. Y.: Doubleday and Co., 1974.

This treatise on early metalware includes tin,
copper, pewter, brass, iron, and bronze from all
over the world. Of interest to the smith are examples of trivets, lighting devices, kitchen utensils, and tools which are found occasionally
throughout the book. 191 pp., ill., bibliog., ind.

Peterson, Harold L. American Indian Tomahawks. Con-
tributions From the Museum of the American Indian
Heye Foundation, vol. 19. New York: Museum of the
American Indian Heye Foundation, 1971.

This is a detailed study of the various types of
tomahawks used in America over the past 250 years.
Over 300 examples are illustrated, including belt
axes, hammer poll types, pipe tomahawks, spike
tomahawks, and stone axes. Each sample is well
photographed and identified as to size, origin,
and other physical characteristics. The development
of the tomahawk is followed in the text which includes discussions of styles, makers, and users.
Many different methods of manufacture are presented in abundant detail suitable for use by the
smith. 142 pp., ill., bibliog.

Revi, Albert Christian, ed. Spinning Wheel's Collec-
tible Iron, Tin, Copper, and Brass. Secaucus, N. J.:
Castle Books, 1974.

This is a series of reprints from the pages of
Spinning Wheel magazine on a variety of metal
products of early American origin. Of interest to
blacksmiths are articles on wrought iron collecting, trivets, lighting devices, hatchets, and

hardware. These are among over fifty articles and are necessarily brief, only touching upon the surface of the subject in most cases. 158 pp., ill.

Russell, Carl Parcher. _Firearms, Traps, and Tools of the Mountain Men_. New York: Alfred A. Knopf, 1967.

This is a comprehensive and voluminous treatise on the various iron and steel accoutrements of the early American trappers, traders, and Indians. Drawings and documentation are provided for a number of articles, including knives, spear points, traps, fire steels, axes, tomahawks, and firearms with comments on the range and time of their use and importance to their users. In addition, the frontier blacksmith is discussed, profiles of known smiths are presented, and the tools and equipment used are described. This book is the most thorough and definitive work in the area of blackpowder and Western fur-trade smithy written 458 pp., ill., bibliog., ind.

Sloane, Eric. _A Museum of Early American Tools_. New York: Ballantine Books, 1964.

This collection of antique tools is protrayed in excellent sketches with descriptive text. It includes a wide variety of tools made by the blacksmith such as axes, hammers, wedges, froes, drawknives, chisels, gouges, nails, knives, and auger bits. The pieces are dated, making the information suitable for reproduction work. 108 pp., ill., ind.

Sonn, Albert H. Early American Wrought Iron. New York: Charles Scribner's Sons, 1928. Reprint (3 vols. in 1). New York: Bonanza Books, 1979.

This outstanding record of Colonial and Early American ironwork, presented in three volumes of sketches, is considered the most comprehensive study ever printed on the subject. The work is illustrated by plates of charcoal drawings with each article identified as to location found, and date of origin, and any unusual characteristics are noted.

Volume 1 covers door hardware, including knockers, Suffolk and Norfolk style latches, lifts and bars, latch locks, and locks.

Volume 2 deals with hinges, hasps, and sliding bolts.

Volume 3 includes weather vanes, wall anchors, gutter supports, foot scrapers, sash fixtures, andirons, fireplace accessories, kitchen utensils, lighting devices, gates, grills, and railings.

This book is very useful to the smith for the reproduction of early ironwork, as well as for ideas in techniques and methods of construction. 131 pp., 731 pls., bibliog., ind.

Vince, John. Old Farm Tools. Shire Album 4. Aylesbury, Bucks, U. K.: Shire Publications, 1974.

Antique British farm tools are presented in captioned photographs with descriptive text showing the tools and their uses for a variety of jobs. Many blacksmith-produced tools include cultivating and harvesting implements, digging tools, and pruning and weeding devices. 32 pp., ill.

Wrot Iron Designers, The. _Art_ _in_ _Iron_. New York: The
Wrot Iron Designers, 1932.

This is a multivolume set of wrought iron design
books containing sketches of a variety of forged
articles, including doors, gates, railings, grills,
lighting devices, fireplace accessories, furniture,
hardware, and assorted architectural commissions.
Motifs are developed according to country, and
traditional patterns are relied upon heavily,
especially scrollwork. Approx. 300 unnumbered pp.,
ill.

15. Religious Ironwork

Bergmann, A. <u>Die</u> <u>Schmiedekreuze</u> <u>der</u> <u>Oberpfalz:</u> <u>Der</u>
<u>Westen</u> <u>und</u> <u>der</u> <u>Süden</u>. Kallmunz, Germany: Lassleben,
1972.

    This is a study of several dozen wrought iron
crosses from gravesites, displaying varying degrees
of skill and complexity. Text in German. 11 pp.
text, 41 pls.

Bergmann, A. <u>Die</u> <u>Schmiedekreuze</u> <u>der</u> <u>Ostoberpfalz:</u>
<u>Zwischen</u> <u>der</u> <u>Naab</u> <u>und</u> <u>dem</u> <u>Oberpfalzer</u> <u>Wald</u>. Kallmunz:
Lassleben, 1970.

    This volume contains over eight examples of
wrought iron crosses from gravesites, representing
varying degrees of complexity from simple scroll
work to intricate floral arrangements. Some closeups of details are included. Text in German.
31 pp. text, 13 pls.

Jonsson, Oscar. _Smidda Jarnkors: Paeksharads Kyrko-gard_. Introduction by Brynolf Hellner. Nordiska Museets Handlingar, vol. 1. Stockholm: P. A. Norstedt and Soner, 1932.

> This booklet presents over 100 drawings of Swedish grave markers from the eighteenth and nineteenth centuries. Nineteen pages of text in Swedish. 52 pp., ill.

Kühn, Fritz; Schindler, Ernst; and Di Michiel, M. L. _Sakrale Schmiedekunst: Schmiedearbeiten in der Kirche und auf dem Friedhof_. Colemanns Entwurfsmappen für das metallverarbeitende Handwerk series, vol. 10. Lübeck: Charles Colemann, Verlag, 1968.

> These working drawings of contemporary German ironwork suitable for churches include candle sconces, screens, grillwork, and a variety of crosses. 36 pp., ill.

16. European Architectural Ironwork

Abel, Gustave. <u>Salzburger Gitter</u> erzählen: <u>Kleine</u>
<u>Metaphysik schmiedeeiserner Kunst</u>. Salzburg, Austria:
M M Publishers, 1965.

    This brief historical survey of Austrian iron-
work emphasizes architectural elements of grills
and gates in twenty-five examples. Text and captions in German. 66 pp., ill.

Battachi, Franco, Jr. <u>Il Ferro battuto</u>. Milan: Ulrico
Hoepli, 1971.

    This voluminous pictorial treatise on the grill-
work, gates, stair railings, lighting devices,
furniture, and fireplace accessories throughout
Italy's history includes contemporary executions.
Well photographed with text and captions in Italian. 228 pp., ill.

Batacchi, Franco. <u>Schmiedeeisen für Haus und Garten</u>.
Milan: G. Gorlich, 1970.

    These contemporary and traditional ironwork
panels, gates, grills, stairways, and lighting
devices are presented through photographs in some
cases and working drawings in others. Descriptions

of photographs in German. Text pages unnumbered,
100 pls.

Baur-Heinhold, Margarete. Geschmiedetes Eisen: Vom
Mittelalter Bis um 1900. Taunus, Germany: Hans Koster
Konigstein, 1963.

This volume depicts traditional European grillwork, gates, stairways, and other ornamental architectural wrought ironwork from the middle ages
through 1900. Descriptions in German. 112 pp., ill.

Brüning, Adolf/Rhode-Hamburg, Alfred. Monographien
des Kunstgewerbes. Leipzig: Von Klinkhardt und Bier-
mann, 1922.

This history of European architectural ironwork
has a German text and 171 illustrations. It contains examples of ornamental gates and screens
from all periods of European history. 160 pp.,
ill., ind.

Byne, Arthur, and Stapley, Mildred. Spanish Ironwork.
N.p.: Hispanic Society of America, 1915.

This is a lengthy treatise on the history and
development of Spanish ironwork from the 13th
through the 19th centuries. It covers architectural
pieces and the smaller functional hardware and
household accessories, including locks, door
knockers, and chest ironwork. Text in English.
143 pp., ill., ind.

Casalgrande, Alfredo. <u>Nuove</u> <u>Cancellate</u>: <u>Ringhiere,</u>
<u>Balcone,</u> <u>Chiusure,</u> <u>Scale,</u> <u>Inferriate,</u> <u>ecc.</u> <u>in</u> <u>Ferro</u>
<u>Lavorato</u>. Cuneo, Italy: Industrie Grafiche Italiane,
1961.

   This book presents 188 contemporary drawings of
   design suited for ornamental ironwork of gates,
   stairways, fences, and grill panels, most of
   which are clearly intended for electric and gas
   welding fabrication. 188 diagrams.

Clouzot, Henri. <u>La</u> <u>Ferronnerie</u> <u>Moderne</u>: <u>A</u> <u>L'exposition</u>
<u>Internationale</u> <u>des</u> <u>Arts</u> <u>Decoratifs</u>. Paris: Charles
Moreau, 1927.

   These are photographs of contemporary French
   wrought ironwork as of the mid 1920s. Examples
   include gates, grills, railings, lighting devices,
   furniture, and screens chosen for elaborate, ornate
   form and sophisticated execution in thirty-eight
   plates with French captions and introduction.

Fayet, Monique de. <u>Ferronnerie</u> <u>Espagnole</u>. Paris:
Charles Massin, 1969.

   This pictorial collection of traditional Spanish
   ironwork, including gates, grills, balconies, furniture, and keys; well, door, and fireplace hardware; lighting devices and music stands, from the
   thirteenth to the eighteenth centuries, is presented in 132 illustrations. Captions in French
   and Spanish. 72 pls.

Gatz, Conrad, ed. <u>Wrought</u> <u>Iron</u> <u>Railings,</u> <u>Doors,</u> <u>and</u>
<u>Gates</u>. Architect's "Detail" Library, vol. 1. Trans-
lated by E. H. F. Ostarhilde. London: Illiffe Books,
1964.

This photographic study of contemporary Western
utilitarian railings, screens, fences, doors, balconies, and stairways contains very few examples
of forge work. Text describes the illustrations.
It would be useful to the smith as a source of
ideas for forge work, as many of the examples
could be applied as motifs by the smith. 119 pp.,
ill.

Geerlings, Gerald K. <u>Wrought</u> <u>Iron</u> <u>in</u> <u>Architecture:</u>
<u>Wrought</u> <u>Iron</u> <u>Craftsmanship:</u> <u>Historical</u> <u>Notes</u> <u>and</u>
<u>Illustrations</u> <u>of</u> <u>Wrought</u> <u>Iron</u> <u>in</u> <u>Italy,</u> <u>Spain,</u> <u>France,</u>
<u>Holland,</u> <u>Belgium,</u> <u>England,</u> <u>Germany,</u> America; <u>Modern</u>
<u>Wrought</u> <u>Iron;</u> <u>Lighting</u> <u>Fixtures</u> <u>and</u> <u>Knockers,</u> <u>Speci-</u>
<u>fications</u>. 1929. Reprint. New York: Crown Publishers,
Bonanza Books, 1957.

This scholarly treatise on wrought ironwork's
history and development in various Western cultures
is intended to teach patrons of ironwork how to
appreciate, select a design, and specify an execution intelligently. The text is accompanied by
324 photographs and scale drawings of railings,
stairways, balconies, gates, grillwork, and other
architectural pieces from Europe, Great Britain,
and America. The volume contains a chapter on
tools and design considerations, and one on lighting fixtures and door knockers. 202 pp., ill.

Hellner, Brynolf. Jarnsmidet: i Vastidens dekorativa konst. Stockholm: Nordiska Museet, 1948.

This volume depicts sixteenth- and seventeenth-century ironwork of Scandinavia, including grills, gates, lighting devices, door hardware, locks, and strong box hardware, presented in 173 pls, with Swedish text.

Hellner, Brynolf, and Rooth, Sune. Konstsmide: historia och teknik. Stockholm: Victor Pettersons, 1960.

This voluminous history of ironwork contains illustrations of European ironwork arranged by periods from the earliest times, with a section on modern Scandinavian architectural ironwork. In Swedish. 348 pp., ill., bibliog., ind.

Heintschel, H. Schmiedeeisen/Wrought Iron. Innsbruck, Austria: Pinguin Publishers, 1973.

This pictorial survey of Alpine ironwork from the 14th to the 18th centuries consists mainly of architectural pieces, including gates and grills, but also covers crosses, doors, hardware, utensils, chests, and clocks. Text in English and German. 104 pp., ill.

Hoever, Otto. Encyclopedia of Ironwork. 1927. Reprinted as Wrought Iron: Encyclopedia of Ironwork. New York: Universe Books, 1962.

This pictorial survey of European grills, gates, lanterns, and door knockers covers the twelfth to the eighteenth centuries in 320 plates. The original title was Das Eisenwerk (1927); the Spanish edition, Hierros Artisticos (1929) has an Introduction by George Kowalczyk. 33 pp., ill.

Kastner, Otfried. Handgeschmiedet: eisenkunst in Osterreich aus der zeit der Landnahme, Romanik und Gotik. Linz, Austria: J. Wimmer, Publisher, 1967.

Ornate German wrought iron grills, gates, door hardware, strongboxes, hinges, hasps, and lanterns of the fifteenth and sixteenth centuries are depicted in 127 illustrations with German captions. 308 pp., ill., bibliog.

Kastner, Otfried. Schmiedehandwerk im Barock: Renaissance, Manierismus, Knorpelwekstil, Hochbarock (Blumenstil, Laub- und Bandlwerkstil), Regence, Rokoko und Louis XVI. Linz: J. Wimmer, Verlag, 1971.

This collection of Austrian wrought ironwork from the sixteenth through the eighteenth centuries includes screens, gates, grillwork, crosses, and sign brackets. It contains 178 examples of ironwork with text and descriptions in German. 309 pp., ill.

Kühn, Fritz. Eisen und Stahl. Leipzig: E. A. Seemann, 1957.

This design book of wrought ironwork is intended to illustrate the processes involved in smithing, from idea through design, drawing, and execution, to finished piece. It illustrates the tools and some of the processes and then gives working drawings and photographs of the executions. This book is a notable contribution to the production of quality wrought ironwork. Text is in German. 199 pp., ill.

Kühn, Fritz. Schmiedekunst: Geschichte eines Handwerks.
Lübeck: Charles Coleman, Verlag, 1968.

This is a photographic survey of selected historical architectural ironwork in Germany and a
series of executions of master smith Fritz Kühn.
Examples are presented on design and artistic merit
rather than historical importance. Examples include
grills, screens, gates, doors, and stairways. Text
and captions are in German. 36 pp., ill.

Kühn, Fritz; Schindler, Ernst; and Di Michiel, M. L.
Balkon-und Brüstungsgitter. Colemans Entwurfsmappen
fur das metallverarbeitende Handwerk series, vol. 4.
Lübeck, Charles Coleman, Verlag, 1965.

This book presents designs and working drawings
with dimensions of contemporary German railings
and grills in iron and steel. 8 pp. and 32 pls.

Kühn, Fritz; Schindler, Ernst; and Di Michiel, M. L.
Puertas Enrejadas. Edited by Gustavo Gili. Barcelona:
Gustavo Gili, 1972.

This is a Spanish edition of Coleman's Handwerk
series, containing sketches and working drawings
of contemporary German gates and hinged screens,
including details of affixture and dimensions.
Text is in Spanish and German. 7 pp. and 32 pls.,
ill.

Kühn, Fritz; Schindler, Ernst; and di Michiel, M. L.
Trenngitter im Raum. Colemans Entwurfsmappen für das
metallverarbeitende Handwerk series, vol. 5. Lübeck:
Charles Coleman, Verlag, 1966.

This volume contains working drawings of contemporary German dividers and grillwork in steel,

forged iron, and bronze with dimensions and construction details. 6 pp. and 32 pls., ill.

Kühn, Fritz; Schindler, Ernst; and di Michiel, M. L. Treppen-Geländer. Colemans Entwurfsmappen für das metallverarbeitende Handwerk series, vol. 2. Lübeck: Charles Coleman, Verlag, 1968.

   This volume of designs and working drawings for contemporary German stairways includes railings and grill panels in steel, forged iron, and bronze presented with stock dimensions and construction details. 8 pp. and 32 pls., ill.

Labarta, Luis. Hierros Artisticos: Colleccion de Laminas Representando los Mas Notables Trabajos de Forja, Particularmente los Debidos a los Maestros Castellanos y Catalanes. Barcelona: Franco Seix, 1901.

   This pamphlet contains a variety of historical ironwork executions from France and Spain presented in a series of charcoal drawings. Examples covered include gates, railings, lighting devices, door hardware, keys, hinges, and handles from the eleventh to the seventeenth centuries in 100 plates with Spanish and French captions. 16 pp. and 100 pls., ill.

Lecoq, Raymond. Ferronnerie ancienne. Paris: Charles Massin, 1961.

   This is a book of photographs of architectural and domestic wrought ironwork of France from the twelfth to the eighteenth centuries. Examples include grillwork, door hardware, railings, gates, andirons, trivets, keys, lighting devices, and furniture in thirty-six plates. 36 pp.

Meyer, Franz Sales. _Die Schmiedekunst_. Seemanns Kunstgewerbliche Handbucher, vol. 2. Leipzig: E. A. Seemann, 1888.

This survey of German ironwork, including tools and some technique, was basically intended to acquaint a general readership with the work of the smith. It contains drawings of gates, sign brackets, grills, lock plates, hinges, candle holders, and door knockers. It is of use primarily for the design of pieces, as the text is in Greman. 204 pp., ill., bibliog.

Mora, Vincente Nadal. _La Herreria Artistica del Buenos Aires Antiguo_. Buenos Aires: Comisión National de Museos y Monumentos Históricos, 1957.

This volume contains drawings of architectural executions, including window grills and gates, with emphasis on design details taken from traditional Argentinian examples. It includes some working dimensions of the pieces. Text is in Spanish. 160 pp., ill.

Odenhausen Helmuth. _Gitter aus Stahl: in neuen Formen_. Dusseldorf: Stahleisen, G.m.b.H., 1962.

This book on modern German architectural ironwork consists of photographs of gates, railings, security screens, stairways, and room dividers in a variety of forged and fabricated designs and patterns. 211 pp., ill., ind.

Oirschot, Anton van. _Antiek Kopen_. Helmond, Belgium: Uitgeverij, 1969.

This is a photographic survey of Belgian wrought iron from Roman times to the nineteenth century.

It covers architectural work, lighting devices,
tools, weapons, chests, fireplace accessories, and
domestic articles. The text is in Dutch, but the
many illustrations are useful and self-explanatory
as a source of design examples from this period
and location. 143 pp., ill., bibliog., ind.

Poillerat, Gilbert. Ferronnerie D'aujourd'hui. Paris:
Charles Moreau, 1951.

These photographs of twentieth century French
ornamental furniture, lighting devices, andirons,
grills, doors, and small gates are presented in
forty-eight examples with introduction and captions
in French. 5 pp.

Robl, Franz. Schmiedeeisen. Leipzig: Eiserne Hammer,
1940.

Traditional German architectural ironwork, including gates, stair railings, balconies, and room
dividers is presented in forty-seven photographs.
The book also contains a few nonarchitectural executions including a candelabrum and an iron cross.
Text is in German. 36 pp., ill.

Scheel, Hans. Schmiede- und Schlosserarbeiten: Ges-
taltete Arbeiten aus Stahl, Sondermessing und Leichtmetall. 2 vols. Stuttgart: Julius Hoffman, 1959, 1965.

This pictorial survey of contemporary European
ironwork, including lighting devices, grills,
gates, fireplace accessories, crosses, and room
dividers also contains some working drawings of
architectural executions. Text is in German.
Vol. 1: 168 pp., ill., ind. Vol. 2: 168 pp., ill.,
ind.

Sierra, Alfonso de. Forja Marroqui: Teoria do la Voluta. Cuadernos de Arquitectura Popular Marroqui, vol. 1. Tetuan, Spain: Marroqui, 1956.

This history and development of Spanish ironwork is presented in Spanish text with many sketches and working drawings of grills, gates, and panels, primarily using scrollwork. It is of use to the smith for designs of the classic Spanish-type scroll work. 185 pp., ill.

Smetana, Gunther. Entwürfe für Kunstschmiedearbeiten. Stuttgart: Julius Hoffman, 1955.

This volume presents a series of excellent working drawings of wrought ironwork with many closeup construction details of fastenings. The book includes designs of grills, gates, various lighting devices, and hardware. It is highly recommended as a source of practical construction solutions specifically addressed to the smith. 180 pp., 102 pls.

Valk, H. Tallinna sepis: N.p., 1972.

This collection of ninety-four photographs represents the wrought ironwork of the northern European city of Tallinn from the sixteenth through eighteenth centuries. Examples include weather vanes, sign brackets, wall anchors, gargoyles, doors and door hardware, grills, locks, and keys. 94 pp., ill.

Zimelli, Umberto, and Giovanni, Vergerio. Decorative Ironwork. New York: Paul Hamlyn, 1966.

This volume presents examples of European architectural ironwork from antiquity to the twentieth century arranged into principal art periods. It

is intended for art historians rather than blacksmiths as the examples shown are rather lavish and
ornate. 157 pp., ill.

17. British Architectural Ironwork

Ayrton, Maxwell, and Silcock, Arnold. <u>Wrought</u> <u>Iron</u> <u>and</u> <u>Its</u> <u>Decorative</u> <u>Use</u>. New York: Charles Scribner's Sons, 1929.

    This historical treatise on British ironwork from Roman times through the eighteenth century is arranged by era and locality. It contains many photographs of architectural executions from all periods covered, substantiated by analysis of the literature of the period in the text. 196 pp., ill., ind.

Chatwin, Amina. <u>Cheltenham's</u> <u>Ornamental</u> <u>Ironwork:</u> <u>A</u> <u>Guide</u> <u>and</u> <u>History</u>. Cheltenham, U. K.: 1974.

    This history of and guide to the ironwork in this British city includes gates, railings, and grills, both cast and wrought, and text discussing the makers and their patrons. 91 pp., ill., ind.

Gardner, John Starkie. English Ironwork of the seventeenth and eighteenth Centuries: An Historical and Analytical Account of the Development of Exterior Smithcraft. 1911. Reissued. New York: Benjamin Blom, 1972.

This volume covers architectural ironwork, such as gates, railings, grills, and sign brackets. The development of gates is followed from earliest examples to the work of Jean Tijou and other gate-smiths, discussing their evolution, style, and influences. The text is supplemented by 162 illustrations. 373 pp., 88 pls.

Gardner, John Starkie. Ironwork. 3 vols. London: Chapman and Hall, 1893-1922.

Vol. 1, From the Earliest Times to the End of the Mediaeval Period, covers the manufacture and working of iron throughout the world, including blacksmithing, locksmithing, and the influences of the Crusades. Presented in well-written text with fifty-seven illustrations. 152 pp., ind.

Vol. 2, Being a Continuation of the First Handbook, and Comprising From the Close of the Mediaeval Period to the End of the Eighteenth Century, Excluding English Work, covers Italian, German, Dutch, and French Renaissance ironwork and baroque and rococco ironwork in France. The extensive text is accompanied by 133 illustrations of examples. 202 pp., ind.

Vol. 3, The Artistic Working of Iron in Great Britain from the Earliest Times, is a history of ironwork in Great Britain covering the production of the material, the effects of the earliest influences, the major periods including medieval and Renaissance, the work of Jean Tijou, and cast ironwork. The text is supplemented by fifty-five illustrations. 197 pp., ind.

Goodwin-Smith, R. English Domestic Metalwork. Leigh-on-Sea, Essex, U. K.: F. Lewis, Publishers, 1937.

This extensive pictorial study of British wrought ironwork includes gates, grills, door hardware, lighting devices, fireplace accessories, kitchen utensils, and grill work, which are presented in drawings and photographs of historic originals and modern reproductions. Each section has text descriptive of the articles illustrated, with commentary on the influences, techniques, and variations of the designs. 101 pp., 139 pls.

John Harris, comp. English Decorative Ironwork: From Contemporary Source Books 1610-1836: A Collection of Drawings and Pattern Books Including a New Booke of Drawings by John Tijou, 1693; A New Book of Iron Work by J. Jores, 1756; The Smith's Right Hand by W. and J. Welldon, 1765; Ornamental Iron Work by I. and J. Taylor, c. 1795; A Book of Designs by J. Bottomley, 1793; etc. Chicago, Ill.: Quadrangle Books, 1960.

This book covers architectural ironwork in Great Britain from 1610 to 1836 with commentary and reproductions of the drawings and pattern books of the smiths of that period. It is an excellent source of designs and examples from this period. 19 pp. and 168 pls., ind.

Hollister-Short, G. J. Discovering Wrought Iron.
Tring, Herts., England: Shire Publications, 1970.

This history of British wrought ironwork from
medieval times to the nineteenth century includes
influences, styles, the periods, and some of the
principle smiths when known. Some photographs and
drawings accompany the text. 71 pp., ill., ind.

Lindsay, John Seymour. An Anatomy of English Wrought
Iron. New York: Taplinger Publishing Co., 1965.

This is a historical survey of the influences on
and development of English ironwork. Each major
period is discussed and illustrated with important
contributions of the time. Examples include grills,
gates, railings, hinges, latches, and door knockers.
Supplemental surveys include tools and operations
of the forge, twist patterns for bars, and leaf
work. The illustrations are excellent line and
charcoal drawings. 58 pp., 178 ill., ind.

Lister, Raymond. Decorative Wrought Ironwork in Great
Britain. N.p.: G. Bell and Sons, 1957; Rutland, Vt.:
Charles E. Tuttle Co., 1970.

This detailed history of British ironwork is
intended to increase general audience appreciation
for the techniques and development of the art. It
contains sections on technique, architectural and
domestic ironwork. Influences of the major periods
in history from Roman times to the present are
covered, following the changes in style from period
to period. 280 pp., 28 pls.

Small, Tunstall, and Woodbridge, Christopher. English
Wrought Ironwork: Mediaeval and Early Renaissance, A
Portfolio of Full Size Details. New York: William
Helburn, 1931.

   This portfolio contains twenty plates of working
   drawings and full-size details of early English
   hinges, railings, latches, handles, casement fas-
   teners, and knockers, intended for the use of the
   blacksmith. 20 pls.

Small, Tunstall, and Woodbridge, Christopher. English
Wrought Ironwork of the Late Seventeenth and Early
Eighteenth Centuries: A Portfolio of Full-Size Details.
New York: William Helburn, 1930.

   This portfolio contains twenty examples of
   famous British ironwork, including gates, railings,
   screens, door brackets, and ornaments with both
   leaf and flower work, presented in working drawings
   and full-size details. 20 pls.

Twopeny, William. English Metal Work: Ninety-Three
Drawings. Preface by Laurence Binyon. London: Archibald Constable and Co., 1904.

   This is an excellent collection of charcoal
   drawings of wrought iron door hardware and railing
   standards with some lead and cast iron work included. It particularly emphasizes door knockers
   and handles. Even though dimensions are omitted,
   the style of the artist strongly suggests the feel
   of wrought iron. 93 ill.

Victoria and Albert Museum. A Picture Book of English
Wrought Ironwork. London: Waterlow and Sons, 1926.

    This booklet contains twenty examples of English
    ironwork from medieval times to the late eighteenth
    century, including grills, gates, and railings,
    presented in photographs. 2 pp. text, 20 pls.

18. American Architectural Ironwork

Artcraft Ornamental Iron Co. <u>Art</u> <u>in</u> <u>Iron</u>: <u>A</u> <u>Refer-</u><u>ence</u> <u>Book</u> <u>of</u> <u>Wrought</u> <u>Ironwork</u> <u>for</u> <u>Architects</u>, <u>Build-</u><u>ers</u>, <u>and</u> <u>Home</u> <u>Owners</u>. Columbus, Ohio: 1947.

    This catalogue is a series of sketches illus-
trating the products of this ornamental iron company. The designs are simple, standard, and well-
suited to cold forming. Some details are forged
and some are cast from iron, brass, or aluminum.
The selection includes grills, balconies, railings,
support brackets, and mail box standards. 22 pp.,
ill.

Cervantes, Enrique A. <u>Hierros</u> <u>de</u> <u>Oaxaca</u>. Oaxaca,
Mexico: N.p., 1932.

    This is a series of drawings of ornamental iron-
work, including railings and stair railings, of
Colonial Mexico presented in forty-two plates with
captions in Spanish.

Curtis, Mrs. Elizabeth Gibbon. Gateways and Doorways
of Charleston, South Carolina, in the Eighteenth and
the Nineteenth Centuries. Edited and Introduced by
Maxwell Kimball and Arthur C. Holden. New York:
Architectural Book Publishing Co., 1926.

These photographs of gates, railings, stairways,
and doorways include many interesting designs in
wrought iron. 67 pp., ill.

Deas, Alston. The Early Ironwork of Charleston. Introduced by Albert Simons. Columbia, S. C.: Bostick and
Thornley, Publishers, 1941.

These drawings and descriptions of a variety of
gates, grills, balconies, sign brackets, foot
scrapers, and shutterguards of Charleston, South
Carolina, cover the colonial period up to the mid-
1800s. The text explores the development and influences of design and execution. 111 pp., ill.,
bibliog., ind.

Delcroix, Eugene. Patios, Stairways, and Iron Lace
Balconies of Old New Orleans. Introduced by Stanley
Clisby Arthur. New Orleans: Harmanson, Publisher,
1938.

These photographs are primarily of architectural
cast iron work but a couple of wrought iron gates
are worth noting. 92 pp., ill.

Fiske, J. W. Illustrated Catalogue of Artistic Wrought
Iron, Brass, and Bronze Work: Area Gates, Window
Guards, Transoms, Grills, Railing Posts, Etc. New
York: N.p., 1891.

These are excellent engravings of a variety of
architectural ironwork designs executed by the New

York firm of J. W. Fiske. Heavy use of scrolls and plant forms are illustrated on such executions as doors, window grills, gates, railings, stairways, and newel posts. The volume is primarily useful for designs, as most details of construction are omitted. 278 pls.

Garcia, Luis Islas. Hierros Forjados. Coleccion Ana-huac de Arte Mexicano, vol. 18. Mexico City, D. F.: Ediciones de Arte, 1948.

This is a series of photographs of Colonial Mexican ironwork, including gates, grills, railings, crosses, and balconies, presented in forty-seven examples with introductory text and captions in four languages including English. 69 pp., ill.

Monroy, Salazar. Forja Colonial de Puebla. Mexico: N.p., 1946.

These drawings of Colonial Mexican architectural and domestic wrought ironwork include gates, balconies, stairways, lock escutcheon plates, keys, door hardware, chest ironwork, spurs, and light-ing devices. Introductory text in Spanish. 113 pp., ill.

Renner and Maras, Inc. Wrought in Metal. New York: N.p., 1932.

The catalogue of selected executions by this firm was intended to give customers guidelines for selecting work and to impart a sense of the range of possibilities extant in forged iron, bronze, and monel metal. Examples include grills, gates, stairways, balconies, doors, and screens presented

in photographs with some closeup details of
repoussé and floral forging. 36 pls.

Wallace, Phillip B. <u>Colonial</u> <u>Ironwork</u> <u>in</u> <u>Old</u> <u>Phila-</u>
<u>delphia</u>. 1930. Reprint. New York: Dover Publications,
1970.

This is a collection of photographs and working
drawings of gates and railings of Colonial Philadelphia. It contains a brief section on foot
scrapers. It is an excellent source of reference
material for the period covered. 148 pp., ill.,
ind.

Winslow Brothers Co. <u>Artistic</u> <u>Metalwork</u>. Chicago,
1943.

This is a catalog with scale drawings and sketches
of ornamental architectural metal work executed in
a variety of locations by the Winslow Brothers
Company. It includes heavily scrolled railings,
grills, gates, elevators, stairs, light fixtures,
and hinge work made primarily in iron but also in
bronze and brass. 33 pls.

Winslow Brothers Co. <u>Collection</u> <u>of</u> <u>Photographs</u> <u>of</u>
<u>Ornamental</u> <u>Iron</u> <u>Executed</u> <u>by</u> <u>the</u> <u>Winslow</u> <u>Bros.</u> <u>Co.</u>
Chicago, 1893.

This is an extensive photographic collection of
architectural decorative wrought ironwork executed
by the Winslow Brothers Company. Architectural
executions include elevator screens, lanterns,
grills, gates, balconies, stair railings, and sign
brackets. Decorative executions include candelabra,
stands, door knockers, fireplace accessories, and
wall tables employing a rich variety of scroll

work, animal forms and various flowers and leaves.
141 pls.

19. Work of the Masters

Accrocca, Elio Filippo. Antonio D'Andrea. Italy: De Luca, n.d.

    This is a photographic collection of the work of blacksmith D'Andrea executed in Italy during the 1940s and 1950s. Examples include repoussé panels, fireplace accessories, lighting devices, grill-work, sculpture, and animal forms presented in 101 plates. Text in Italian.

Bergmeister, Manfred. Bronze + Stahl: Schmiedearbeiten. Bad Worishofen, Germany: Hans Holzmann, 1970.

    This book presents sculptural and ornamental wrought ironwork and bronzework including gates, doors, panels, and free-standing sculpture by the German artist/smith, Manfred Bergmeister. Text in English. 123 pp., ill.

Edwards, Ifor. Davies Brothers Gatesmiths: Eighteenth-Century Wrought Ironwork in Wales. Cardiff, Wales: Welsh Arts Council/Crafts Advisory Committee, 1977.

    This is a study of the work of the eighteenth century Welsh master gatesmiths Robert and John Davies. Their work is documented, illustrated, and

tied into the overall influences of the period.
Photographs of the gates are accompanied by closeups of the details and characteristic motifs they
employed. 109 pp., ill., bibliog.

Kühn, Fritz. Geschmiedetes Gerät. Tübingen: Ernst
Wasmuth, 1954. Translated: Decorative Work in Wrought
Iron and Other Metals. London: Harrap and Co., 1967.

These photographs and working drawings of the
work of Fritz Kuhn include lighting devices, bowls,
furniture, crosses, door hardware, fireplace accessories, and lettering in steel, iron, and bronze.
392 pp., ill.

Kühn, Fritz. Kunst der Gestaltung. Düsseldorf: Stahleisen, G.m.b.H., n.d.

This photographic collection of sculptural and
functional ironwork by master smith Fritz Kühn
includes grillwork, crosses, railings, panels, and
free-standing art work make by forging and chemical treatment. 46 pp., ill. Text in German.

Kühn, Fritz. Wrought Iron. London: George C. Harrap
and Co., 1965.

This volume presents numerous photographs of the
forge work of Fritz Kühn, including an extensive
an extensive series of detailed closeups of individual forged elements such as scrolls, twists,
panel motifs, methods of connection, and stylistic
natural forms. It contains many examples of screens,
grills, gates, and railings. 120 pp., ill.

Laufer, Gunther. Schmiedearbeiten. Germany: Institut
für Angewandte Kunst, 1958.

This pamphlet presents nineteen photographs of
the ironwork of Gunther Laufer, executed in the
early 1950s. Examples include screens, lighting
devices, and door hardware. Text in German. 16 pp.,
ill.

Rehme, Wilhelm. Ausgeführte Moderne Kunstschmiede-
Arbeiten. Berlin: Baumgartner's, n.d.

This series of photographs and sketches of the
Art Nouveau architectural ironwork of Wilhelm
Rehme includes railings, grills, doorways, gates,
hinges, and balconies. The sketches often are complete enough to show the intended method of fabrication and are useful as working drawings for the
smith. 106 pp., ill.

Roth, Edwin. Neue Schmiedeformen. Munich: D. W.
Callwey, 1962.

This volume pictures contemporary sculptural and
functional architectural ironwork designed by the
author and executed in a number of smithies. Includes room dividers, grills, gates, and railings.
Captions in German. 251 pp., ill.

Schmirler, Otto. Der Kunstschmied. Tübingen: Ernst
Wasmuth, Publisher, 1976.

This volume is a collection of drawings and
photographs of the work of master smith Otto
Schmirler and his shop. The abundant display of
articles includes grills, balconies, window
screens, gates, furniture, fireplace accessories,
railings, lighting devices, and miscellaneous

indoor and outdoor hardware. Details of animal and plant forgings, sketches showing attachments of fixtures, and working dimensions further enrich the content. This is an excellent source of traditional and contemporary German design useful to the practicing smith and student. 224 pp., ill.

20. Exhibition Catalogues

Art Gallery of Ontario. <u>Wrought Iron</u>: <u>European</u> House-
<u>hold</u> <u>Utensils</u> <u>from</u> <u>the</u> <u>Seventeenth</u> <u>to</u> <u>the</u> <u>Nineteenth</u>
<u>Century</u>. Introduction by Richard J. Wattenmaker.
Ontario, Canada: Extension Services, Art Gallery of
Ontario, 1975.

In this catalogue selected entries from the
MacDonald Stewart Collection, Montreal Military
and Maritime Museum, St. Helen's Island, Montreal,
are illustrated, including trammels, trivets, cook-
ing utensils, lighting devices, and toasters.
30 pp., ill., bibliog.

Davis, Myra Tolmach. <u>Sketches</u> <u>in</u> <u>Iron</u>: <u>Samuel</u> <u>Yellin</u>,
<u>American</u> <u>Master</u> <u>of</u> <u>Wrought</u> <u>Iron</u>, <u>1885-1940</u>. Introduc-
tion by Evelyn Stolte. Washington, D. C.: George
Washington University, 1971.

This illustrated biography of the life and work
of Samuel Yellin was prepared for a 1971 exhibition
at the Dimock Gallery in Washington, D. C. It
describes Yellin's life, the importance and scale
of his work, illustrates his shop and workers, and
some of his executions. The booklet concludes with

a list of major commissions and bibliography.
31 pp., ill., bibliog.

University Museum and Art Galleries, Southern Illinois
University, Carbondale. Iron, Solid Wrought / USA.
Carbondale: Southern Illinois University, 1976.

This is the catalogue of a 187-entry exhibit
with many of the pieces well illustrated. Historical American ironwork is presented, including the
tools, hardware, furniture, and agricultural implements of a growing nation. Invitational and sub-
mitted entries by contemporary smiths include
tools, sculpture, architectural pieces, hardware,
fireplace and kitchen accessories, and furniture.
Introduced by Alex Bealer with text by B. E.
Retzinger, L. Brent Kington, and Evert A. Johnson.
72 pp., ill.

University of St. Thomas Art Department. Made of Iron.
Houston: University of St. Thomas, 1966.

This catalogue of the 515 entries exhibited includes illustrations of many of the pieces. It
covers ironwork chronologically from earliest
times to the present and from many parts of the
world. Objects include religious talismans, tools,
sculpture, weapons, hardware, utensils, and armor,
fashioned by forging and cold working. It contains
introductions by Cyril Stanley Smith, Stephen V.
Grancsay, and John de Menil. 288 pp., ill.,
bibliog.

Indexes

Author Index

Title Index